دُدِ الْهُوياتِ و التَنكُراتِ
لِلْجَماعَةِ المُسَمّاةِ الْمُهاجِرُوْنَ

A Critical Study of the Multiple Identities and Disguises of 'al-Muhajiroun'

The organisation known as "The Salafi Youth for Islamic Propagation"

Exposing the antics of the cult followers of Omar Bakri Muhammad Fustuq!

By Abū Ameenah 'AbdurRahmān as-Salafī and 'AbdulHaq ibn Kofi ibn Kwesi al-Ashantī

Forewords by Shaykh, Dr Abū Bakr Thānī (Aqeedah Department, Islamic University of Madeenah), Umar Jamaykee (Imām of Brixton Mosque) and Hamza Bajwa (News Editor of the Muslim Weekly newspaper)

دراسة نقدية لتعدد الهويات و التنكرات للجماعة المسماة المُهاجرون

A Critical Study of the Multiple Identities and Disguises of 'al-Muhajiroun'

The organisation known as
"The Salafi Youth for Islamic Propagation"

Exposing the antics of the cult followers of Omar Bakri Muhammad Fustuq!

ISBN 978-0-9551099-4-2
© Jamiah Media
All Rights Reserved
2009 CE/1430 AH
Published by Jamiah Media
Authors: Abū Ameenah 'AbdurRahmān as-Salafī and 'AbdulHaq al-Ashantī
Email: admin@salafimanhaj.com

1

Contents

بسم الله الرحمن الرحيم

إن الحمد لله، نحمده ونستعينه ونستغفره، ونعوذ بالله من شرور أنفسنا
ومن سيئات أعمالنا، من يهده الله فلا مضل له، ومن يضلل فلا هادي له،
وأشهد أن لا إله إلا الله وحده لا شريك له ، وأشهد أن نبينا محمداً عبد
الله ورسوله، صلى الله عليه وعلى آله وأصحابه ومن اقتفى أثره.

أما بعد، فقد اطلعت على الكتاب الذي ألفه الأخوان العزيزان أبو أمينة
عبد الرحمن السلفي وعبد الحق الأَشَانتي وألفيته قيماً في موضوعه وفي
المسائل التي عالجها، وموفقاً في عرضه ونقده، وقوياً في رده للأسس
والعقائد التي بني عليها فكر التكفيريين وأتباع حزب التحرير وما تنطوي
عليه من الأباطيل، وخصوصاً في وجهها القبيح الذي يظهر به في الدول
الغربية، وإن كانت المدرسة من حيث أصولها كلها واحدة في العالم،
تركيزها تكفير المجتمعات وحكامها ، ونظرة مشؤومة تجاه ما عليه الأمة،
وإساءة الظن بعلمائها، بل وتكفيرهم، مستلهمين تلك الأفكار من
المدرسة الأم مدرسة بن لادن والزرقاوي وأبي قتادة وأبي محمد المقدسي
وغيرهم ممن تزعم الكلام على المسائل المدلهمة دون الأخذ بمنهج العلماء.
وقد تتبع الأخوان منهج رموز هؤلاء وأثبتا بإنصاف ما هم عليه من سوء
طوية وجهل كبير بأصول الدين ومنهج سلف الأمة، وكشفا عن بُعْدِهم

3

عن علم الدين والعلماء، وكذبهم بادعاء العلم، وعدم صلاحيتهم للكلام باسم المسلمين في دُوَلهم. وقد افتتن بهؤلاء كثير من شباب المسلمين في شتى أنحاء العالم، ثاروا على مجتمعاتهم، وصاروا سبباً لتوجيه التهم للإسلام والمسلمين، وأعطوا الكفار فرصة الهجوم على الإسلام وتعاليمه وعلمائه ومناهج دراسته، حتى صار شغل كثير من قادة العالم محاولة القضاء على تعاليم الإسلام باسم محاربة الإرهاب، بذريعة ، بل بتعاون من هؤلاء الذين لا علم عندهم.

فبدل أن يكونوا دعاة خير إلى الإسلام ببيان محاسنه لأهل المجتمعات التي يعيشون فيها، وبأخلاق طيبة هي من أسس دينهم، صاروا حرباً على دينهم وعلى أهلهم بسلوك منهج الخوارج الذين لا يرون خيراً في أحد لا يحمل باطلهم.

وأسأل الله تعالى أن يبارك في هذا الجهد وينفع به المسلمين، ويبصر به عقول شبابنا ويردهم عن الافتتان بتلك المناهج المبتدعة، ويقي الأمة شرورَها، وأن يجمع كلمة المسلمين في الدول الغربية وفي العالم كله على الحق الناصع الذي في منهج السلف الصالح الذي لا يصلح آخر هذه الأمة إلا به .

وصلى الله وسلم وبارك على نبينا محمد وعلى آله وعلى أصحابه أجمعين.

وكتبه:

أبو بكر محمد ثاني

قسم العقيدة الجامعة الإسلامية بالمدينة المنورة

2-6-1430هـ

In the Name of Allah, The Most Beneficent, The Most Merciful

All praise is due to Allāh, we praise Him, we seek His aid, and we ask for His forgiveness. We seek refuge in Allāh from the evil of our actions and from the evil consequences of our actions. Whomever Allāh guides, there is none to misguide and whomever Allāh misguides there is none to guide. I bear witness that there is no god worthy of worship except Allāh and I bear witness that our noble Prophet Muhammad is the servant and messenger of Allāh. May Allah's *salah* and *salam* be upon him, his family, his companions and those who follow his footsteps.

I have read through the treatise written by brothers Abu Ameenah Abd Ar-Rahman As-Salafi and Abd Al-Haqq Al-Ashanti and found it to be well written, rich in information on what it touches upon and it hits the nail on the head in exposing the fundamental tenets of the takfiri movements in the Western world and the UK in particular.

Takfiri trends now transcend all geographical boarders under different guises. Their main concern is to declare the whole Ummah as disbelievers especially the rulers of the Muslim countries. Claiming to be offshoots of the *Salafi Da'wah* they indulge mainly in discussing political issues and the ailing situation of the Muslim Ummah and its predicaments, they then metamorphose into hard-line takfiris that see nothing good in the Muslim communities and their rulers, due to their ignorance of the fundamentals of Islam in the light of the Qur'an, the Sunnah and the understanding of the Salaf, but instead, tracing the steps of the new-age Takfiri leaders like Bin Ladin, Zarqawi, Abu Qatadah, Abu Muhammad Al-Maqdisi and their likes who had revolted against the Muslim Ummah and declared its scholars and rulers as infidels.

These people, knowingly or not, are the real cause of the present bad situation of the Muslim Ummah, as they have given the Western countries and almost all rulers the excuse to molest and maltreat the Muslims, create chaos in all Muslim countries, and be weary of the teachings of Islam in their own countries, in the name of fighting terrorism. That is because these so-called activists indulge into acts of terrorizing their communities thereby causing non-Muslims to hate Islam and what it stands for. I may not be far from the fact if I boldly assert that these people are actually being used to give this tragic picture of Islam.

These people should have become good ambassadors of Islam by calling people in the West to its beautiful teachings in the best manner and showing, by example, its main mission in terms of Tauheed, etiquettes, goodness to neighbours, goodness to one's own community and to humanity as a whole.

Brothers Abu Ameenah and Abd Al-Haqq have truly exposed the reality of these takfiri leaders in the persona of Umar Bakri and his followers and established beyond any iota of doubt the ignorance of these pseudo-shaikhs of the deen of Islam and that they have no right whatsoever to speak on behalf of the Muslims or be regarded as representing the Muslims in their communities.

I hope this book will go a long way in enlightening our youth and make them return to the right path as taught by our pious predecessors, and shun the innovated trends of the Khawarij, and may Allah save our various Muslim communities and countries from the evil of these destructive movements.

Wa salla Allahu ala Nabiyyina Muhammadin wa 'ala aalihi wa Sahbihi Ajma'in.

Abubakar Muhammad Sani (Phd. Aqeedah)
Department of Aqeedah
Islamic University of Madeenah
02-06-1430 AH/ 26-05-2009 CE

FOREWORD BY UMAR AL-JAMAYKĪ
(GRADUATE FROM FACULTY OF HADEETH, MADEENAH UNIVERSITY AND
IMAM OF BRIXTON MOSQUE, LONDON)

Verily all praise is for Allāh, we praise Him and seek His aid and ask for His forgiveness, and we seek refuge with Allāh from the evils of ourselves and our evil actions. Whomever Allāh guides there is none who can misguide him, and whomever Allāh misguides there is none who can guide him, and I bear witness that none has the right to be worshipped except Allāh Alone, having no partner, and I bear witness that Muhammad is His slave and His Messenger. May the Salāt and Salaam be upon Prophet Muhammad (*SallAllāhu 'alayhi wa Sallam*), his family, his companions, and all those who follow him until the Last hour.

﴿يَا أَيُّهَا الَّذِينَ آمَنُواْ اتَّقُواْ اللَّهَ حَقَّ تُقَاتِهِ وَلاَ تَمُوتُنَّ إِلاَّ وَأَنتُم مُّسْلِمُونَ﴾

"O you who have believed, fear Allāh as He should be feared and do not die except as Muslims (in submission to Him)."
{Āli-Imrān (3): 102}

﴿يَا أَيُّهَا النَّاسُ اتَّقُواْ رَبَّكُمُ الَّذِي خَلَقَكُم مِّن نَّفْسٍ وَاحِدَةٍ وَخَلَقَ مِنْهَا زَوْجَهَا وَبَثَّ مِنْهُمَا رِجَالاً كَثِيرًا وَنِسَاء وَاتَّقُواْ اللَّهَ الَّذِي تَسَاءلُونَ بِهِ وَالأَرْحَامَ إِنَّ اللَّهَ كَانَ عَلَيْكُمْ رَقِيبًا﴾

"O mankind, fear your Lord, who created you from one soul and created from it its mate and dispersed from both of them many men and women. And fear Allāh through whom you ask things from each other, and (respect) the wombs. Indeed Allāh is ever, over you, an Observer."
{an-Nisā (4): 1}

8

يَا أَيُّهَا الَّذِينَ آمَنُوا اتَّقُوا اللَّهَ وَقُولُوا قَوْلًا سَدِيدًا

يُصْلِحْ لَكُمْ أَعْمَالَكُمْ وَيَغْفِرْ لَكُمْ ذُنُوبَكُمْ وَمَن يُطِعْ اللَّهَ وَرَسُولَهُ

فَقَدْ فَازَ فَوْزًا عَظِيمًا

"O you who have believed, fear Allāh and speak words of appropriate justice. He will amend for you your deeds and forgive your sins. And whoever obeys Allāh and His Messenger has certainly attained a great attainment."
{al-Ahzāb (33): 70-71}

Verily, the most truthful speech is the book of Allaah. The best guidance is the guidance of Muhammad (sallAllāhu 'alayhi wa Sallam). The worst of affairs are the newly-invented ones, and every newly-invented matter is an innovation. Every innovation is a misguidance and every misguidance is in the Fire. To Proceed:

I have read the book written by our two esteemed brothers Abu Ameenah AbdurRahmān as-Salafī and AbdulHaqq al-Ashantī which gives a critical study of this present day sect led by Omar Bakri Muhammad and those that follow him. The book is a long awaited research shedding some light on their erroneous ideas and understanding on some very crucial topics on matters of Islamic Creed and Fiqh facing the Ummah today.

This book intends to outline and refute the false approach which they are upon and give the true reality of their Da'wah which is that of the takfīrī methodology, such as holding the Muslim rulers to be disbelievers on account of them falling into certain sinful actions. Their approach has no true resemblance to the way of Ahlus-Sunnah and the way of Salaf us-Sālih, yet in recent times they have hidden under the name of Salafiyyah to tarnish the Beauty of this Daw'ah.

I fully encourage the need for such research which refutes and exposes the falsehood of this sect and their misrepresentation of Islām in the eyes of the general public. This work fully deconstructs their teachings which poison the mind of our youth by playing upon their emotions and lack of knowledge on various Islamic matters.

With this humble effort of our brothers the futility of this sect and their false principles have been clarified so that the truth may become clear and the falsehood they represent be exposed. May Allāh accept their effort and Guide us all wa Billahi Tawfik.

Umar al-Jamaykī
Graduate from Madeenah University, Faculty of Hadeeth Studies and Imām of Masjid Ibn Taymiyyah (Brixton Mosque and Islamic Cultural Centre, London)
Friday 29 May 2009 CE/5 Jumādā ath-Thānī 1430 AH

FOREWORD BY HAMZA A. BAJWA
(WRITER AND NEWS EDITOR OF THE MUSLIM WEEKLY)

Immediately following the September 11 terror attacks upon the United States in 2001, it was aphoristically said that the airliners used in the suicide attacks were not the only things hijacked that day - Islam too had been hijacked.

In response to the assault, the US subsequently invaded and occupied Afghanistan and Iraq in what was part of the infamously dubbed 'War on Terror'. This was reinforced by a concurrent informational war initiated by certain agenda-driven western organisations and think-tanks. The objective was not just to identify an enemy to lay the immediate blame on, but to use the attacks as an excuse to isolate and negatively stigmatise all Muslim groups perceived to be anti-western and said to have some influence towards the supposed ideological underpinnings of 'terrorism'. Inexcusably, the Salafi (*Salafiyyah*) group – pejoratively labelled by their enemies as Wahhabis (*Wahhabiyyah*) – was also included. Since then, a concerted effort has been made by these defamers to mendaciously link terrorism and its ideological framework to Salafism in general, and, by extension, Saudi Arabia for institutionally establishing Salafism. It could be said, therefore, that a more accurate rendition of the aforementioned aphorism should have been restricted appropriately to Salafism having been hijacked.

Noticeably, however, these calumnies are not just limited to non-Muslims. During the past few years, a vocal anti-Salafi Muslim faction (vacuously lauding itself as moderate, liberal traditionalists) has sinisterly reared its ugly head to follow suit. In contrast, as these malicious attacks on Salafism have intensified, a paradoxical trend has emerged where some Muslim groups have disingenuously adopted either some of the more distinguishable Salafi precepts and traits or the very title itself, despite holding and propagating overtly antithetical Salafi practices.

Omar Bakri and his motley crew are notorious for their constant theological shifts and chameleon-like changes, especially since the London bombings in July 2005. This has been soundly exemplified by two radical changes on the part of Bakri's *Al-Muhajiroun*: Firstly, their adoption of external features distinct to a practicing Salafi, such as, the beard (having finally realised that allowing the beard to grow in resemblance of their Prophet [upon whom be peace] is obligatory) and the outer garment (the *thawb*). Secondly, their unjustified usurpation of the Salafi 'tag' as a title, e.g. *'The Salafi Youth for Islamic Propagation, 'Salafi Media'* and *'The Salafi Youth*

11

Movement'. This has, predictably, caused not just a degree of confusion and misunderstanding for the uninformed, but also provided more ammunition for the anti-Salafi movement to further muddy the waters.

It is in this confused milieu, in which the extremism of *Al-Muhajiroun* is wrongly being conflated with Salafism, that books similar to '*A Critical Study of the Multiple Identities and Disguises of al-Muhajiroun*' are so urgently needed. Hence, this book is particularly illuminating, *masha'Allaah*, since its authors Abū Ameenah 'AbdurRahmān as-Salafī and 'AbdulHaq al-Ashantī of SalafiManhaj.com peel back the layers to clarify how far removed this cult is from correctly understanding and implementing Salafism. Sadly, it is unfortunate that a greater volume of critical responses in the English language of a similar high standard have not been produced and widely circulated by the western-based Salafis.

Of course, this is not true of the Salafi scholars, especially the many residing in Saudi Arabia, who are not just renowned intellectual giants; but have been at the forefront of the Islamic theological 'War on Terror'. Again, however, their efforts in combating and rebutting the poisonous ideology that fuels terrorism and extremism has been largely confined to the Muslim world with little of it being translated over for access in the West.

Although the small numbers of Western-based Salafis, restricted by the limited resources at their disposal, have been somewhat slow out of the blocks, there are definite signs of improvement. In this context, SalafiManhaj.com has quite noticeably, and in short time, acquired a formidable reputation in publishing a variety of works directly countering this anti-Salafi propaganda. It has, in effect, single handedly raised the bar for all other Salafi organisations to aim for and emulate. However, in the face of such a real and present threat and increasing hostility, what the Salafis must guard against is a culture of passivity, apathy, or worse still, silence. This would only be to their detriment.

Hamza A. Bajwa
News Editor of *The Muslim Weekly* (www.themuslimweekly.com)

Summary

The aim of this study is to diametrically separate the Salafis from the deviant group *al-Muhajiroun* which since its inception has transformed into a number of guises under the tutelage of Omar Bakrī Muhammad. The study will explore the underlying beliefs and claims of the cult with a view to understanding its core tenets. The study looks at the wider issues related to the *takfiri* movements and their main beliefs. Our research has also explored a wide range of websites which have content related to the persona of Omar Bakrī, this has been all the more important considering his expulsion from the UK, which then led him to increase his web-based propagation including Pal-talk lectures to his cult followers from *al-Muhajiroun*.

A clear link between *al-Muhajiroun* and other new-age *takfīrī* activists is immediately noticeable and we have brought attention to this within this study. It will also be evident that the cult followers of Omar Bakrī apparently began using the term "Salafī" due to a number of factors. One of these factors culminates in an endgame to somehow assimilate the finer principles of the Salafī method, without violating their own innovated, controversial peculiarities, and thus gain victory over the hearts and minds of the Muslims. History has taught us that mimicking the truth in order to establish an ulterior agenda has always been the most effective way to beguile a people. The core beliefs and methods of Omar Bakrī and *al-Muhajiroun* consist mainly of the following:

- ✓ *Polarising Tawheed ul-Hākimiyyah as an independent category*
- ✓ *Takfeer of the Muslim rulers with neither consideration of the relevant conditions of takfeer nor maintenance of the preventative factors.*
- ✓ *Full blame placed on the Muslim rulers for the calamities which befall the Muslim Ummah.*
- ✓ *Contradictory dealings with non-Muslims along with simplistic views on Muslim and non-Muslim relations.*
- ✓ *Support for the likes of Bin Laden, Zarqawi, Abu Qatada and others.*
- ✓ *Praise of terrorists in order to agitate.*
- ✓ *Participation in protests, marches and demonstrations, and all of this opposes the juristic rulings of contemporary Salafī scholars.*

13

There are many other differences between mainstream Salafis and the followers of Omar Bakrī Muhammad whatever their guise. The book also undertakes the task to provide an accurate account of their mutations and evolutionary traits, in both matters of creed and methodology. From the days when they were clean-shaven, Levi jeans sporting juveniles - shouting slogans such as "khilāfah" at the top of their voices; up till the present day when they have gowned the majestic attire of the Sunnah, and have embraced numerous qualities of the Salafīs. It is also astonishing how they manage to reconcile their contempt for the Salafīs, whilst at the same time, steadily absorbing and assimilating their traits - not just in action but also in name. The level of irony in this is amusing - to say the least.

Our primary fieldwork involved a variety of face-to-face interactions and discussions with active followers of Omar Bakrī Muhammad in Luton and East London where they are the most active and vocal. We also had the opportunity of posing questions to them when followers of Bakri attempted to propagate their views in Brixton on Saturday 25 April 2009. In the vibrant, and sometimes heated, confrontation a few brothers challenged the followers of Omar Bakrī on issues such as: unrestricted *takfeer* of Muslims; the scholarly credentials of Omar Bakrī; their ignorance of Arabic and their lack of knowledge of Usūl ul-Fiqh. Anjem Choudhary was also present and failed to respond adequately to these question posed, he and others from their followers can be approached to ascertain the veracity of what occurred in Brixton on that day.

We also found that mainly the Salafis were directly challenging *al-Muhajiroun* and Omar Bakrī with the role of others being minimal. We also found that while Omar Bakrī promotes his beliefs and views actively in English, there is nothing at all which indicates that he is active, popular or even known among Arab youth. The cult following of Omar Bakrī is largest in East London and Luton with there being little cult followers in other cities, let alone in other countries. Al-Muhajiroun is also based in other UK cities such as Birmingham, Cardiff, Stoke-on-Trent, Slough and some of the northern cities.

14

RESEARCH RESTRICTIONS

Some material from websites linked to *al-Muhajiroun* and Omar Bakrī was abruptly removed and key articles, books and papers were taken off the Internet. This made it difficult to quote from them as some material could no longer be found.

Due to the followers of Omar Bakrī constantly being in flux it was noticed that they would change their views, beliefs and methods in order to be in line with the latest mood that Omar Bakrī may happen to be in, this can be seen in their new-found calls to Salafiyyah.

THANKS & APPRECIATION

Firstly, we would like thank Allāh, the Glorious & Majestic, all praise is due to Him. We then have to extend our thanks to: Abū 'Ubayd Khālid ibn Fitzroy Knight, the moderator of SalafiManhaj.com, for his notable graphic design efforts; Zulfikār al-Atharī, who took his time out while during his exams at Madeenah University to inform his teachers of the project; 'Abdul-Haqq Baker for his overall support despite his busy schedule in Saudi Arabia and with his PhD; Abū Fātimah Azar and Abū Idrees for proof-reading. May Allāh increase them all in goodness and grant them success in this life and the next.

Narrated 'Abdullāh Ibn 'Amr Ibn al-'Ās *(radi allāhu 'anhu)*: "I heard Allāh's Messenger *(sallallāhu alayhi wasallam)* saying: *"Allāh does not take away the knowledge by taking it away from (the hearts of) the people, but He takes it away by the death of the scholars till when none of the (scholars) remains, people will take as their leaders ignorant people who when consulted will give their verdict without knowledge. So, they will go astray and will lead the people astray."*[1]

Abū Hurayrah *(radi Allāhu 'anhu)* narrated that the Messenger of Allāh *(sallallāhu alayhi wassallam)* said: *"There will come upon the people years of deceit wherein the liar will be regarded as truthful and the truthful will be considered a liar and the dishonest will be trusted and the trustworthy one will be considered dishonest and the Ruwaybidah will begin to speak!"* Then it was asked: *"What are the Ruwaybidah?"* He *(sallallāhu alayhi wassallam)* replied: *"The foolish insignificant man who speaks about general affairs."*[2]

INTRODUCTION

Indeed, all praise is due to Allāh, we praise Him, we seek His aid, and we ask for His forgiveness. We seek refuge in Allāh from the evil of our actions and from the evil consequences of our actions. Whomever Allāh guides, there is none to misguide and whoever Allāh misguides there is none to guide. We bear witness that there is no god worthy of worship except Allāh and that Muhammad is the servant and messenger of Allāh.

﴿يَا أَيُّهَا الَّذِينَ آمَنُواْ اتَّقُواْ اللَّهَ حَقَّ تُقَاتِهِ وَلاَ تَمُوتُنَّ إِلاَّ وَأَنتُم مُّسْلِمُونَ﴾

"O you who have believed, fear Allāh as He should be feared and do not die except as Muslims (in submission to Him)."

{Āli-Imrān (3): 102}

﴿يَا أَيُّهَا النَّاسُ اتَّقُواْ رَبَّكُمُ الَّذِي خَلَقَكُم مِّن نَّفْسٍ وَاحِدَةٍ وَخَلَقَ
مِنْهَا زَوْجَهَا وَبَثَّ مِنْهُمَا رِجَالاً كَثِيرًا وَنِسَاء وَاتَّقُواْ اللّهَ الَّذِي
تَسَاءلُونَ بِهِ وَالأَرْحَامَ إِنَّ اللّهَ كَانَ عَلَيْكُمْ رَقِيبًا﴾

"O mankind, fear your Lord, who created you from one soul and created from it its mate and dispersed from both of them many men and women. And fear Allāh through whom you ask things from each other, and (respect) the wombs. Indeed Allāh is ever, over you, an Observer."

{an-Nisā (4): 1}

$$\text{﴿يَا أَيُّهَا الَّذِينَ آمَنُوا اتَّقُوا اللَّهَ وَقُولُوا قَوْلًا سَدِيدًا}$$

$$\text{يُصْلِحْ لَكُمْ أَعْمَالَكُمْ وَيَغْفِرْ لَكُمْ ذُنُوبَكُمْ وَمَن يُطِعْ اللَّهَ وَرَسُولَهُ}$$

$$\text{فَقَدْ فَازَ فَوْزًا عَظِيمًا﴾}$$

"O you who have believed, fear Allāh and speak words of appropriate justice. He will amend for you your deeds and forgive your sins. And whoever obeys Allāh and His Messenger has certainly attained a great attainment."

{al-Ahzāb (33): 70-71}

To proceed:

The *tadlees* (deception) of the Bakrī fraternity seems to know no end, from the British law expert and second-in-command Anjem Choudhary claiming to be an "Islāmic judge" to Omar Bakrī claiming to be a scholar and a Salafi, now it has emerged that some of his followers have set up an organisation entitled the **"Salafi Youth for Islāmic Propagation"** (aka the **"Salafi Youth Movement"** and the **"Salafi Youth Association"**). As a result, this study hopes to assess the claims of this newly fangled organisation and one audacious claim particularly, that they are the true adherents to the Salafi methodology. It has reached us that the following has recently been advertised:

http://www.dailymail.co.uk/news/article-1054909/Have-babies-Muslims-UK-hate-fanatic-says-warning-comes-9-11-UK.html

The one seated in the middle who goes by the name **"Saiful-Islām"** also known as **"'AbdulHādī"**[3] (from Luton)[4] claims to be the head of the so-called **"Salafi Youth for Islāmic Propagation"**, while the one on the far right is one of Omar Bakrī's overzealous supporters in Luton. They even had a projected picture of their "Shaykh" Omar Bakrī in the background to provide the whole lecture with an ambience of authenticity.[5] Strangely, "Saiful-Islām" (aka "'AbdulHādī") of the so-called "Salafi Youth for Islāmic Propagation" when questioned by a Salafi brother in East London promptly denied Bakrī's scholarly status over his band of merry men, saying **"he's not my Shaykh"**. Why the abrupt denial when it is widely known among the Muslims that Bakrī is their main reference point for Islāmic issues? Could it have anything to do with the recent exposure (as it were!) of Omar Bakrī and what his own hands have reaped? Indeed, here "Saiful-Islām" (aka "'AbdulHādī"), after 3 minutes and 30 seconds makes clear reference to "Shaykh" Omar Bakrī and also praises Abū Qatādah as being a "Shaykh", along with referring to others: http://uk.youtube.com/watch?v=7DegNdjhqCk&feature=related In Brixton on Saturday 25th April 2009 "Saiful-Islām" (aka "'AbdulHādī") then went back on this and claimed that we, the authors, have lied on him in regards to his denial of Bakrī. Well, we therefore ask Allāh to curse whoever is lying!

The cult is also famed for its sanctimonious calls for wanting the "Sharee'ah" implemented. As for their alleged call to want the *Sharee'ah* implemented, then if the cult really understood the *Sharee'ah* then they would be the last to advocate *Sharee'ah*, if they knew what *Sharee'ah* would do to them and their fitnah-making and sedition! The irony is that they call for a thing which would, in reality, dismantle and dispose of them. So it is not about just loving the *Sharee'ah*, it is also about loving the 'prophetic' way by which we can establish the *Sharee'ah*. They may claim to love the *Sharee'ah*, but this claim lacks conviction because they refuse to use the Prophetic methodology to resurrect that which they claim to love. Allāh says,

$$﴿قُلْ إِن كُنتُمْ تُحِبُّونَ اللَّهَ فَاتَّبِعُونِي يُحْبِبْكُمُ اللَّهُ وَيَغْفِرْ لَكُمْ ذُنُوبَكُمْ وَاللَّهُ غَفُورٌ رَّحِيمٌ﴾$$

"Say, [O Muhammad], "If you should truly love Allāh, then follow me, [so] Allāh will love you and forgive you your sins. And Allāh is Forgiving and Merciful.""

{Āli 'Imrān (3): 31}

Ibn Katheer (*rahimahullāh*) states about this virtuous *ayah* of the Qur'an:

This honorable Ayah judges against those who claim to love Allāh, yet do not follow the way of Muhammad. Such people are not true in their claim until they follow the Sharee'ah (Law) of Muhammad and his religion in all his statements, actions and conditions. It is

19

recorded in the Sahih that the Messenger of Allāh said in the famous hadeeth in Saheeh Bukhārī from 'Ā'ishah *(radi Allāhu 'anhā)*,

«مَنْ عَمِلَ عَمَلًا لَيْسَ عَلَيْهِ أَمْرُنَا فَهُوَ رَدٌّ»

"Whoever does an action that does not conform with our matter then it will be rejected."

This is why Allāh said here,

﴿قُلْ إِن كُنتُمْ تُحِبُّونَ اللَّهَ فَاتَّبِعُونِي يُحْبِبْكُمُ اللَّهُ﴾

"Say, [O Muhammad], "If you should truly love Allāh, then follow me, [so] Allāh will love you..."

Meaning: what you will earn is much more than what you sought in loving Him, for Allāh will love you. Al-Hasan al-Basrī and several scholars among the *Salaf* commented, "Some people claimed that they love Allāh. So Allāh tested them with this *ayah*:

﴿قُلْ إِن كُنتُمْ تُحِبُّونَ اللَّهَ فَاتَّبِعُونِي يُحْبِبْكُمُ اللَّهُ﴾

"Say, [O Muhammad], "If you should truly love Allāh, then follow me, [so] Allāh will love you..."

Allāh then said,

﴿وَيَغْفِرْ لَكُمْ ذُنُوبَكُمْ وَاللَّهُ غَفُورٌ رَّحِيمٌ﴾

"...and forgive you your sins. And Allāh is Forgiving and Merciful."

Meaning: by your following the Messenger, you will earn all this with the blessing of his mission.

Where's the truth in their shallow claims for 'loving the Sharee'ah' when they abandon and disown the Sharee'ah's methodology for restoring the *Sharee'ah* as a ruling entity? So al-Muhajiroun can be called to account for their claim of "wanting the Sharee'ah" and deeming all those who oppose them as being "haters of the Sharee'ah", which is also *takfeer* by the way. Because, as Muslims, we love the *Sharee'ah* but the followers of Omar Bakrī have no idea about the *Sharee'ah* and its nuances as exemplified in their total disregard of what the *Sharee'ah* says about dealing with the Muslim rulers and not revolting against them. It is as if their sum idea of "love of the Sharee'ah" is sticking a few luminous coloured stickers on bus-stops and lampposts around London!

Of the more extreme statements, which we will highlight in this introduction due to its dangerous consequences, is what is found in a lecture entitled 'The Tawāgheet of Saudi Arabia' on the takfīrī neo-khāwarij website of Omar Bakrī's al-Muhajiroun cult followers: Islām4uk.com. The speaker from Luton who refers to himself by the pseudonym 'Abu Turāb', whose real name is 'AbdulQādir,[6] appears to suffer from an extreme condition which we have coined: excessive-compulsive takfeer disorder (ECTD), and is a characteristic of a variety of takfīrīs such as 'Abdullāh Faisal al-Jamaykī. After 37 minutes and 37 seconds into the lecture 'Abu Turāb' from Luton makes takfeer of the Mufti of Saudi Arabia, Shaykh 'Abdul'Azeez Āli Shaykh. After 40 minutes and 50 seconds into the lecture, 'Abu Turāb' says that: **"Saudi Arabia is the leading country of shirk, kufr and bida'"** La hawla wa la quwwata ila billāh! So this jāhil, 'Abu Turāb', is actually claiming that Saudi Arabia is top of the list in calling to shirk, kufr and bida' in the entire world!? So neither the nations of Mushrikeen, whether in Asia or Africa, nor the nations of the people of the book, and neither the Zionist state nor the European secular states come in at first place, but rather Saudi Arabia does according to this cult follower of Omar Bakrī?! The logical conclusion of this is well known to the believers, that they are therefore legitmate targets for assassination. When confronted over this during heated discussion in Brixton on Saturday 25th April 2009, AbdulQādir ("Abū Turāb") lied and tried to say to the Salafis that he did not make this statement, even though it is recorded and has been listened to by many!

The Salaf warned against takfeer, tabdī', and tafseeq of anyone, except with evidence, and they considered doing that as being from the actions of the people of innovation. The Salaf also made a distinction between absolute takfeer or tafseeq (such as complete takfeer or tafseeq due to actions of some of the sects of the people of innovation); and between specific takfeer. The Salaf thus say: not all who say or do kufr or fisq are disbelievers or sinners, until the proofs are established,[7] and this is in following the Divinely Legislated texts which strongly warn against that, such as:
In the Two Saheehs from Ibn 'Umar (radi Allāhu 'anhu) who said: the Messenger of Allāh (sallallāhu 'alayhi wassallam) said:

روي ان رسول الله صلى الله عليه وسلم قال: إذا قال الرجل لصاحبه "يا كافر"
فإنما تجب على أحدهما. فإن كان الذي قيل له كافر فهو كافر. وإلا رجع إليه ما
قال.

"Whenever a man says to his brother: "O kāfir!" then it applies to one of them or it returns to the one who actually said it first."[8]

In the Two Saheehs it is reported that the Messenger of Allāh *(sallallāhu 'alayhi wassallam)* said: *"Cursing a Muslim is sin and killing him is kufr."*[9] He also said *(sallallāhu 'alayhi wassallam): "Whoever accuses a believer of kufr then it is as if he has killed him."*[10]

The first thing we need to expose is this: why the need to point the finger at Saudi Arabia? Indeed, 'Abu Turāb' (AbdulQādir), within his *takfiri* tirade, spoke more against the Muslim countries than he did against America, Israel, Europe and Britain? So this in itself is the most vivid proof of their Khārijiyyah and a clear indication that their arguments are indeed weaker than a spider's house. Why the need to isolate Saudi out in matters of *shirk, kufr* and *bida'*? What made this ignorant young speaker single out Saudi from all other Muslim countries like Pakistan, Turkey or Indonesia? Two things are clear from this statement, which ran unrestricted from his mouth like verbal diarrhoea:

1. Either that the speaker has an agenda which causes him to feign ignorance.
2. Or he is profoundly ignorant of the realities of *shirk* and *kufr.*

In our opinion, which is born out of a type of good suspicion, it's the first of the two possibilities, and the reason why we say this is because how can an individual who gives lectures on matters such as *shirk, kufr* and *bida'*, not be aware of the endeavours which Saudi place on actualizing *tawheed* and eradicating *shirk*? How can this young speaker not be privy to the national curriculum of Saudi which includes such books as *Kitāb ut-Tawheed* and *Thalāthat ul-Usūl*? We challenge this erratic speaker to produce one Muslim country that makes the learning of *tawheed* a part of their national school curriculum. Has this boy ever been to places such as Pakistan, Bangladesh, Turkey or Egypt, where *shirk* is rife amongst the Muslims? As for Saudi Arabia being the leading country in terms of *bida'*, then this is another gross piece of hyperbole, which has no weight in reality. Is this boy seriously trying to convince us that the negligible amount of *shirk* found in Saudi is more prevalent than the *shirk* practiced amongst the Barelvis in Pakistan? Even the slightest amount of contemplation on this deplorable assertion is enough for anyone to reject this emotionally driven rhetoric. Let's look between the pages of the Noble Qur'ān which is printed in the land of Saudi Arabia. If they are the foremost practioners of *bida'* why did they base its translation, meanings and *tafāseer* on the works of the three most well known Imāms of *tafseer*? And on top of that, they gave further elaboration and clarification with narrations of Saheeh Bukhārī and Muslim! Why would a country which is neck-deep in *bida'* go to such an extent in keeping the Qur'ān from any innovated understanding? Let's make the challenge slightly more interesting, and scour the earth for a Qur'ān which is more accurate in its translations and meanings. You might point towards Yusuf Ali's translation, however before you do such, ask yourself, who edited and corrected Yusuf Ali's *tafseer* and liberated it from all weird beliefs and misguided translations? So it begs the question from the thoughtful believer, what would cause this frustrated boy to say such a knee-jerk statement?

Could it be his restricted, error-ridden understanding of *Tawheed* and *Shirk*? Could this piece of hyperbole come from his self indoctrination which has caused him to reduce *Tawheed* to issues surrounding the Rulers? The reality therefore is this; the errors of the rulers have caused him to label the whole country as being the leaders of *shirk, kufr* and *bida'*. Let's do some basic arithmetic, how many rulers could Saudi possibly have had? One, two, five, ten? So this small elite group, and its so called '*shirk*', for some reason weighs more on the scales than the *shirk* committed by millions of Muslims in Pakistan, Bangladesh and Turkey!! This is the line of reasoning he is basically requesting of us to follow, and what a hapless train of thought it is! Millions of Muslims commit *shirk* in Pakistan, Bangladesh, Turkey and Africa by worshiping graves and calling upon the dead and 'Abu Turāb' and Bakrī's other cult followers, want us to place all our efforts on a small elite who actually have not fallen into *shirk*.

Another of their simplistic assertions is that the Prophetic Khilāfah ended on March 3rd 1924 CE!? This simplistic belief not only neglects a thorough assessment of the Islāmic adherence of the Ottoman Empire but also seems to be totally ignorant of the actual history and is based on a romantic ideal. For it may be news to al-Muhajiroun, and by extension *Hizb ut-Tahreer*, that Muhammad Fareed Beg mentioned in his book *Tāreekh ad-Dawlat al-'Uthmāniyyah* [History of the Ottoman State], pp.177-178 in regards to the conqueror of Constantinople Sultān Muhammad al-Fātih bin Murād Beg (b. 835 AH/1432 CE, aka Mehmed the Second), that he used to rule by Yāsiq (which included an amalgamation of political ideals inherited from the Byzantine Caesars) and made *tabdeel* of much of the *Shar'!* Muhammad Fareed Beg states that Muhammad al-Fātih bin Murād:

قال محمد فريد بك المحامي في كتابه "تاريخ الدولة العثمانية" (ص/177 -

178) عند ذكر الترتيبات الداخلية للسلطان محمد الفاتح:

"ووضع أول مبادئ القانون المدني وقانون العقوبات فأبدل العقوبات البدنية

أي السن بالسن والعين بالعين وجعل عوضها الغرامات النقدية بكيفية

واضحة اتمها السلطان سليمان القانوني الآتي ذكره".

Implemented the beginnings of the civil law canon and also that of the punishments, he changed (fa abdala) the capital punishments (i.e. chopping off the hand etc.) and replaced them with monetary fines. Sultān Sulaymān al-Qānūnī completed this legislative process.
11

So Sultān Muhammad al-Fātih lived in the ninth Islāmic century after the Hijrah and it is not known that anyone made *takfeer* of this Sultān of the Ottoman Empire, despite this *tabdeel* which included implementing castration upon rapists and others. Many historians have also recognised this, in regards to the Ottoman Empire Carter V. Findlay states in *The Turks in World History*:

Heir to both the Turko-Mongol tradition of dynastic lawmaking and the Islamic sharia, **both of which also recognized custom as a source of law, the Ottomans sought to hold this heterogeneous system together** by giving judicial responsibility under all kinds of law to the religious judges (kadi)...

Outdoing eastern Turko-Mongol states' attempts to balance Islamic and dynastic law, this Ottoman policy paradoxically gave the Islamic sharia the "highest degree of actual efficiency [effectiveness] which it had ever possessed in a society of high material civilisation" after the Abbasid period while simultaneously maximising the scope for dynastic law (yasa kanun).[12]

The historians Shaw and Shaw state in their book *History of the Ottoman Empire and Moden Turkey*, which is a book which defends the Ottoman Empire:

> The Law: **The idea of the law, as it evolved under the Ottomans, combined traditions from both the Persian and Turkish empires of the past as well as those of Islam as such.** From the Persians came the idea – as developed by the Abbasid caliphs – that the ruler was absolute and that all acts of law and justice were favours emanating from his absolute power. **From the Turks, on the other hand, there came an idea of the supreme law (yasa/yasak)** that the ruler had to enforce with justice regardless of his personal wishes. Paralleling these traditions was the Muslim idea of religious law Şeriat *(Sharee'ah)*, derived from the Koran and early Muslim tradition. Whereas the Şeriat was highly developed in the fields of personal behaviour and community life, **it was never developed in detail for most matters of public law, particularly in regard to state organisation and administration. At best it only provided principles, so that there was room for interpretation and legislation on specific matters by the ruler and his government.** Most Muslim legal theorists recognized the right of the sultan by "sovereign prerogative" *(örf)* to take the initiative and issue secular regulations *(kanun; pl. kavanin)* in matters not covered in the Şeriat. **Thus the Ottoman Islamic community had two laws: the customary law of the sultan *(örf-i-sultani)* and the religious law.**[13]

Juan Cole notes in his book *Colonialism and Revolution in the Middle East: Social and Cultural Origins of Egypt's 'Urabi Movement*:

> **Ottoman reformist thinkers from the sixteenth century on often saw implementation of the kanûn-nâmes, whose administrative genealogy lay in the Mongol yâsa or tribal code, as the key to a revival of Ottoman glory.**[14]

Antony Black states in *The History of Islamic Political Thought: From the Prophet to the Present*:

> **The greatest innovation of the Ottoman State was the development of non-religious law (kanun),** also known as customary law *(örf/'urf)*,

the law of the Sultan, or Ottoman law (kanuni osmani). Here again the Ottomans regularised, extended and codified earlier practice. Most originally, they slotted it into the *Shari'a* system: both types of law were administered by the same courts. **This was based partly on self-conscious respect for a Turco-Mongol tradition of popular law (yasa).**[15]

Sami Zubaida stated in *Law and Power in the Islamic World*:

Halil Inalcik, in a seminal paper, examines the model of rule which lay behind Ottoman legislation. One was the traditional Turkish and Mongol tribal models which required the chief to proclaim a set of rules, based on tradition and custom, and to ensure their impartial implementation, avoiding arbitrary judgements.[16]

Zubaida also states:

It is important to note, however, that in Ottoman practice qadi courts did deal with penal cases, alongside other tribunals, but these courts were required to apply qanun regulations alongside the shari'a.[17]

Zubaida continues:

As we have seen, there was a general reluctance to apply limb-amputation penalties, and the combination of strokes and fines became predominant. **Fines are alien to the shari'a tradition, and early jurists prohibited them explicitly: criminals should not have been able to avoid divinely prescribed punishments by paying fines,** and a few early Ottoman ulama and muftis recognized this principle, though few pressed it. In effect, the Ottoman penal system was geared to fines.[18]

Is this ruling by what Allāh has revealed according to *Hizb ut-Tahreer*, Bakri, his cult followers and the other *takfīrīs*? Blatant incorporation of *yāsiq* of the Mongols! This would necessitate Bakri and the new-age *takfīrī* activists to make *takfeer* of the Ottomans according to their own criteria! This indicates that there are different categories of *tabdeel* along with respective rulings, which are totally neglected by the new-age *takfīrī* activists such as Abdullāh Faysal, Abū Baseer, Abū Qatādah, Omar Bakrī, Sulaymān al-'Ulwān and others. Shaykh ul-Islaam Ibn Taymiyyah said:

"والإنسان متى حلل الحرام المجمع عليه ، أو حرم الحلال المجمع عليه ، أو **بدل الشرع المجمع عليه كان كافراً مرتداً باتفاق الفقهاء** ، وفي مثل **هذا** نزل قوله على أحد القولين: {ومن لم يحكم بما أنزل الله فأولئك هم الكافرون} **أي هو المستحل** للحكم بغير ما أنزل الله .

ولفظ "الشرع" يقال في عرف الناس على ثلاثة معان :

"**الشرع المنزَّل**" : وهو ما جاء به الرسول ، وهذا يجب اتباعه ومن خالفه وجبت عقوبته.

والثاني: "**الشرع المؤوَّل**" : وهو آراء العلماء المجتهدين فيها كمذهب مالك ونحوه ، فهذا يسوغ اتباعه ، ولا يجب ، ولا يحرم .

وليس لأحد أن يلزم عموم الناس به ، ولا يمنع عموم الناس منه.

والثالث: "**الشرع المُبَدَّل**" : وهو الكذب على الله ورسوله ، أو على الناس بشهادات الزور ونحوها ، والظلم البين ؛ **فمن قال: إن هذا من شرع الله فقد كفر بلا نزاع** ، كمن قال: إن الدم والميتة حلال ولو قال: هذا مذهبي ونحو ذلك." ا.هـ .

When a person makes halāl whatever is haraam by consensus, or prohibits whatever is halāl by consensus, or replaces whatever is from the Divine Legislation by consensus - he is a disbelieving apostate by agreement of the fuqahā. With regards to the likes of these people Allāh revealed,

﴿وَمَن لَّمْ يَحْكُم بِمَا أَنزَلَ اللَّهُ فَأُولَـٰئِكَ هُمُ الْكَافِرُونَ﴾

"And whoever does not judge by what Allah has revealed – then it is those who are disbelievers."
{al-Mā'idah (5): 44}

Meaning: the one who makes it lawful to rule by other than what Allāh has revealed. The term 'Shar'' according to the custom of people refers to the following three meanings:

First: ash-Shar' al-Munazzal (the revealed legislation), and this is what the Messenger (sallallāhu 'alayhi wassallam) came with, this has to be followed and whoever opposes it has to be punished.

Second: ash-Shar' al-Mu'awwal (the interpeted legislation), and this is in regards to the views of the Mujtahid scholars such as the madhhab of Mālik and the likes. These can be followed yet it is neither obligatory nor impermissible. It is neither for anyone to obligate the people to follow it nor prevent the generality of the people from it.

Third: ash-Shar' al-Mubaddal (the altered legislation), and this is lying against Allāh and His Messenger, or lying against the people with false testimonies or the like; and clear oppression. So whoever says: "Indeed this (type of altered and distorted legislation) is from Allāh" has disbelieved without dispute, just as the one who says: "Eating the blood and dead flesh of an animal are halaal" even if he says: "this is my madhhab" and the likes.[19]

So Shaykh ul-Islām Ibn Taymiyyah (rahimahullāh) clearly explains that the Shar' al-Mubaddal is not one type which is 'ruling by man-made laws taken from the West', rather there are types, Ibn Taymiyyah said:

"وأما "الشرع المبدَّل" فهو الأحاديث المكذوبة ، والتفاسير المقلوبة ، والبدع المضلة التي أدخلت في الشرع وليست منه ، والحكم بغير ما انزل الله ، فهذا ونحوه : لا يحل لأحد اتباعه"

As for ash-Shar' al-Mubaddal then it is: false ahaadeeth, corrupt tafāseer, misguided innovations which have entered the Shar' and are not from it and (a judge) ruling by other than what Allāh has revealed – these and its likes are not permissible for anyone to follow.[20]

Likewise, the ruling on tabdeel is not merely one ruling or ijmā' rather the rulings depend on the type of tabdeel according to Ahl us-Sunnah. It is also well known that when a judge (or ruler) replaces and alters the Shar' and thus rules by other than what Allāh has revealed he obligates the oppressed with his ruling. Yet the ijmā' of the 'Ulama does not make takfeer

28

of such a judge (or ruler) unless he deems and believes this as being lawful (*istihlāl*) for him to do. So *tabdeel* is divided into three types by the 'Ulama:

First type: Whoever replaces the *Shar'* [Divine Legislation] and attaches it to the *Shar'* out of *ijtihād* or interpretation. Such a person intends the rule of Allāh yet errs and is ignorant, such an individual is excused and is not deemed as sinful if he is a person of *ijtihād*. This type of individual is what Shaykh ul-Islaam Ibn Taymiyyah and Ibn ul-Qayyim called "ash-Shar' al-Mu'awwil".

Second type: Whoever replaces the *Shar'* [Divine Legislation] intentionally yet does not attach this to the *Shar'* and his replacement is neither out of arrogance nor obstinancy to the *Shar'*, rather he believes that it is *harām* to do that yet due to a weakness in him such as bribery, position, hatred of a person or the likes he does it. This type of individual is a sinful criminal and has ruled by other than what Allāh has revealed, yet *takfeer* is not to be made of him except if there is a proof of his *istihlāl* (believing it to be lawful), *istikbār* (arrogance towards Allāh's rule) or *mu'ānadah* (obstinancy to Allāh's rule).

Third type: Whoever replaces the *Shar'* [Divine Legislation] intentionally, neither out of an error nor an interpretation, and attaches this to the *Shar'*, this type of individual is an apostate and disbeliever according to the consensus of the Muslims.

When "Abu Turāb" (AbdulQādir) was confronted on this point in Luton in 2008 he stated "we do not accept this categorisation"!? The question which begs to be asked is who is this "we" he refers to? Is it the royal we, which is a nosism employed by someone of high office? Or is this "we" merely a representation of him and his cult members? The latter of the two seems closer to the truth. Small in words is his audacious statement, but so much it discloses. The first thing which we learn from this statement is his severe case of *hizbiyyah* (partisanship) and blind-allegiance to al-Muhajiroun. Now, no one is claiming that Shaykh ul-Islām Ibn Taymiyyah's words amount to revelation, but to casually dismiss his categorisation on the basis of your group's contemporary, biased opinion, not only undermines his status as one of the greatest scholars of Islam but also provides an insight into the bigoted, emotional allegiance they have forged for themselves. This kind of biased allegiance produces nothing but an insulated, false reality which causes its deluded victims to say and do things, which ultimately, will be the architect of their downfall - in this life and the hereafter. One wonders what kind of knowledge and status this "Abu Turāb" (AbdulQādir) possesses to declare such a statement as, "we do not accept this categorisation" Is he privy to knowledge which contradicts Shaykh ul-Islām Ibn Taymiyyah's classification of the types of *tabdeel*? Or is he himself in a position to perform a level of *ijtihād* to rival this categorisation? Perhaps the reality is, Abū Turāb and his associates need to cast doubt on the various types of *tabdeel,* because acceptance of this classical explanation would do severe damage to their political agenda and render false a large portion of what they represent. If they were forced to accept there are types of *tabdeel* that do not amount to *kufr,* but actually are permissible for the well-being of man, what sort of impact would this have on the direction of their *da'wah*? They invest political currency in the third type of *tabdeel* - just like they did with the innovated category of *al-Hākimiyyah* – and then inflate it until it assumes the sole meaning and definition of *tabdeel.* This is a consistent trait found in the people of innovation – the trend of hand-picking an aspect of Islām which aids their agenda, and then they seperate it from its other integral parts and propagate it as a whole to the Muslims with the hope that it will rally them against Muslim leaders.

Another glaring contradiction is how they refer to Imām Muhammad bin 'AbdulWahhāb and Shaykh Muhammad ibn Ibrāheem *(rahimahumullāh)* as if they were both somehow in agreement with the *takfiri* and *khārijī* views of Omar Bakrī Muhammad! They neither made *takfeer* of the Saudi leaders, with whom they were closely aligned, nor did they consider the Saudi rulers to be **"leaders of shirk, kufr and bida'."** Furthermore, Omar Bakrī Muhammad throughout the 1990s believed that Imām Muhammad Ibn 'AbdulWahhāb revolted and rebelled against the Ottomans and Bakrī preached this all over London! This was before his so-called 're-birth' as an avid follower of Imām Muhammad bin 'AbdulWahhāb! Let's look at the views of Imām Muhammad bin 'AbdulWahhāb in regards to revolting and rebelling against the Muslim rulers. Imām Muhammad ibn 'AbdulWahhāb stated:

> **The Imāms from every Madhhab are agreed concerning the one the forcefully took over a region or regions that he has the ruling of "Imām" in all matters. If this had not been so then the affairs of the**

world would never have been established. This is because for a very long time, before the era of Imām Ahmad till this day of ours, the people have never gathered behind a single Imām. And they do not know anyone from the Scholars who has mentioned that any of the Sharee'ah rulings cannot be correct (effected, implemented) except by the overall Imām (the Khaleefah).[21]

Let's turn to what some Islāmic historians have concurred, as opposed to the mere diatribes of the unqualified![22] Shaykh 'Abdul'Azeez Āl-'AbdulLateef said:

Some opponents of the salafi da'wah claim that Imam Muhammad ibn 'Abd al-Wahhāb rebelled against the Ottoman Caliphate, thus splitting the jamā'ah (main body of the Muslims) and refusing to hear and obey (the ruler).[23]

Imām Muhammad ibn 'AbdulWahhāb said in his letter to the people of al-Qaseem:

وأرى وجوب السمع والطاعة لأئمة المسلمين برّهم وفاجرهم ما لم يأمروا بمعصية الله

ومن ولي الخلافة واجتمع عليه الناس ورضوا به وغلبهم بسيفه حتى صار خليفة وجبت طاعته وحرم الخروج عليه

I believe that it is obligatory to hear and obey the leaders of the Muslims, whether they are righteous or immoral, so long as they do not enjoin disobedience towards Allāh. Whoever has become Caliph and the people have given him their support and accepted him, even if he has gained the position of caliph by force, is to be obeyed and it is harām to rebel against him.[24]

And he also said:

الأصل الثالث : أن من تمام الاجتماع السمع والطاعة لمن تأمّر علينا ولو كان عبداً حبشيّاً ..

One of the main principles of unity is to hear and obey whoever is appointed over us even if he is an Abyssinian slave...[25]

And Shaykh 'Abdul'Azeez Āl-'AbdulLateef said:

وبعد هذا التقرير الموجز الذي أبان ما كان عليه الشيخ من وجوب السمع والطاعة لأئمة المسلمين برّهم وفاجرهم ما لم يأمروا بمعصية الله : فإننا نشير إلى مسألة مهمة جوابا عن تلك الشبهة فهناك سؤال مهم هو : هل كانت " نجد " موطن هذه الدعوة ومحل نشأتها تحت سيطرة دولة الخلافة العثمانية ؟

After stating these facts, which explain that the Shaykh believed it was obligatory to hear and obey the leaders of the Muslims whether they are righteous or immoral so long as they do not enjoin disobedience towards Allāh, we may refer to an important issue in response to that false accusation. There is an important question which is: was Najd, where this call originated and first developed, under the sovereignty of the Ottoman state?

Dr Sālih al-'Abood answered this by saying:

لم تشهد " نجد " على العموم نفوذا للدولة العثمانية فما امتد إليها سلطانها ولا أتى إليها ولاة عثمانيون ولا جابت خلال ديارها حامية تركية في الزمان الذي سبق ظهور دعوة الشيخ محمد بن عبد الوهاب رحمه الله وممّا يدل على هذه الحقيقة التاريخية استقرار تقسيمات الدولة العثمانية الإدارية فمن خلال رسالة تركية عنوانها : " قوانين آل عثمان مضامين دفتر الديوان"يعني : " قوانين آل عثمان في ما يتضمنه دفتر الديوان " ، ألّفها يمين علي أفندي الذي كان أمينا للدفتر الخاقاني سنة 1018 هجرية الموافقة لسنة 1609م من خلال هذه الرسالة يتبين أنه منذ أوائل القرن الحادي عشر الهجري كانت دولة آل عثمان تنقسم إلى اثنتين وثلاثين ايالة منها أربع عشرة ايالة عربية وبلاد نجد ليست منها ما عدا الإحساء إن اعتبرناه من نجد ....

Najd never came under Ottoman rule, because the rule of the Ottoman state never reached that far, no Ottoman governor was appointed over that region and the Turkish soldiers never marched through its land during the period that preceded the emergence of the call of Shaykh Muhammad ibn 'AbdulWahhāb (may Allāh have mercy on him). This fact is indicated by the fact that the Ottoman state was divided into administrative provinces. This is known from a Turkish document entitled *Qawāneen Āl 'Uthmān Mudāmeen Daftar* ad-Deewān (Laws of the Ottomans Concerning what is Contained in the Legislation), which was written by Yameen 'Ali Effendi who was in charge of the Constitution in 1018 AH/1609 CE. This document indicates that from the beginning of the eleventh century AH the Ottoman state was divided into 23 provinces, of which 14 were Arabic provinces, and the land of Najd was not one of them, with the exception of al-Ihsa', if we count al-Ihsa' as part of Najd.[26]

And Dr 'Abdullāh al-'Uthaymeen said:

ومهما يكن فإن " نجداً " لم تشهد نفوذاً مباشراً للعثمانيين عليها قبل ظهور دعوة الشيخ محمد بن عبد الوهاب كما أها لم تشهد نفوذاً قوياً يفرض وجوده على سير الحوادث داخلها لأية جهة كانت فلا نفوذ بني جبر أو بني خالد في بعض جهاها ولا نفوذ الأشراف في بعض جهاها الأخرى أحدث نوعاً من الاستقرار السياسي فالحروب بين البلدان النجدية ظلت قائمة والصراع بين قبائلها المختلفة استمر حادّاً عنيفاً

Whatever the case, Najd never experienced direct Ottoman rule before the call of Shaykh Muhammad ibn 'AbdulWahhāb emerged, just as it never experienced any strong influence that could have an impact on events inside Najd. No one had any such influence, and the influence of Bani Jabr or Bani Khālid in some parts, or the Ashrāf in other parts, was limited. None of them were able to bring about political stability, so wars between the various regions of Najd continued and there were ongoing violent conflicts between its various tribes.[27]

Shaykh 'Abdul'Azeez ibn 'Abdullāh ibn Bāz (may Allāh have mercy on him) said in response to this false accusation:

لم يخرج الشيخ محمد بن عبد الوهاب على دولة الخلافة العثمانية فيما أعلم وأعتقد فلم يكن في نجد رئاسة ولا إمارة للأتراك بل كانت نجد إمارات صغيرة وقرى متناثرة وعلى كل بلدة أو قرية – مهما صغرت – أمير مستقل... وهي

33

إمارات بينها قتال وحروب ومشاجرات والشيخ محمد بن عبد الوهاب لم يخرج على دولة الخلافة وإنما خرج على أوضاع فاسدة في بلده فجاهد في الله حق جهاده وصابر وثابر حتى امتد نور هذه الدعوة إلى البلاد الأخرى...

Shaykh Muhammad ibn 'AbdulWahhāb did not rebel against the Ottoman Caliphate as far as I know, because there was no area in Najd that was under Turkish rule. Rather Najd consisted of small emirates and scattered villages, and each town or village, no matter how small, was ruled by an independent emir.[28] These were emirates between which there were fighting, wars and disputes. So Shaykh Muhammad ibn 'AbdulWahhāb did not rebel against the Ottoman state, rather he rebelled against the corrupt situation in his own land, and he strove in jihad for the sake of Allāh and persisted until the light of this call spread to other lands...[29]

Dr. 'Ajeel an-Nashmī said:

..... لم تحرك دولة الخلافة ساكنا ولم تبدر منها أية مبادرة امتعاض أو خلاف

يذكر رغم توالي أربعة من سلاطين آل عثمان في حياة الشيخ ..

The Caliphate did not react in any way and did not show any discontent or resentment during the life of the Shaykh, even though there were four Ottoman sultans during his lifetime...[30]

Dr. an-Nashmī stated further:

لقد كانت صورة حركة الشيخ محمد بن عبد الوهاب لدى دولة الخلافة صورة

قد بلغت من التشويه والتشويش مداه فلم تطلع دولة الخلافة إلا على الوجه

المعادي لحركة الشيخ محمد بن عبد الوهاب سواء عن طريق التقارير التي

يرسلها ولاتما في الحجاز أو بغداد أو غيرهما ..أو عن طريق بعض الأفراد الذين

يصلون إلى الأستانة يحملون الأخبار .

The view that the Caliphate had of the movement of Shaykh Muhammad ibn 'AbdulWahhāb was very distorted and confused, because the Caliphate only listened to those who were hostile towards the movement of Shaykh Muhammad ibn 'AbdulWahhāb, whether that was via reports sent by their governors in the Hijāz, Baghdad and elsewhere, or via some individuals who reached Istanbul bearing news.[31]

With regard to claims of 'AbdulQadeem Zalloum (the former world head of *Hizb ut-Tahreer* who died in 2003 CE) that the Shaykh's call was one of the reasons for the fall of the Caliphate and that the English helped the Wahhabis to topple it, Mahmood Mahdi al-Istanbūlī says concerning this ridiculous claim:

> This writer should be expected to produce proof and evidence for his opinion. Long ago the poet said:
>
> *If claims are not supported by proof, they are used only by the fools as evidence.*
>
> We should also note that history tells us that the English were opposed to this call from the outset, fearing that it might wake the Muslim world up.[32]

And he says:

والغريب المضحك المبكي أن يتهم هذا الأستاذ حركة الشيخ محمد بن عبد الوهاب بأنها من عوامل هدم الخلافة العثمانية مع العلم أن هذه الحركة قامت حوالي عام 1811 م وأن الخلافة هدمت حوالي 1922 م

> The ironic fact is that this Professor accuses the movement of Shaykh Muhammad ibn 'AbdulWahhāb of being one of the factors that led to the destruction of the Ottoman Caliphate, even though this movement began in 1811 CE and the Caliphate was abolished in 1922 CE.[33]

When we turn to the actual writings of Muhammad ibn 'AbdulWahhāb we find that he stated:

> As for your assertion that we hold Muslims to be disbelievers and your question as to how we do this and how we do that, I would simply say that we have never held the Muslims to be disbelievers. Rather, we never held anyone except polytheists to be disbelievers.[34]

In a letter to Muhammad ibn 'Eid, one of the religious personalities of Tharmada, Imām Muhammad ibn 'AbdulWahhāb stated:

> As for the assertion of the enemies that I hold them to be disbelievers only by conjecture, or I hold an ignorant person against

35

whom no argument has been established to be a disbeliever, it is a sheer lie and false accusation, leveled by those who intend to drive the people away from the deen of Allāh and His Messenger.[35]

The Imām also stated (rahimahullāh) in a letter exonerating himself from fabrications concocted by Ibn Suhaym:

Allāh knows that the man ascribed to me what I never said and did not even occur to me. One such ascription is that "the people for the last six hundred years had not been on the right path" and that I hold anyone who seeks the intercession of pious people to be a disbeliever" and that I hold al-Busayree to be a disbeliever. My answer to all of these is: these are nothing more than false accusations![36]

In a letter to the Shareef of Makkah at the time, Imām Muhammad ibn 'AbdulWahhāb stated:

As for falsehoods and accusations, their example is the assertion that we hold the people to be disbelievers in general; that we hold migrating to us obligatory and that we affirm the disbelief of a person who neither holds to what we do nor fights with us. These, and other such assertions, are totally false and have been leveled against us in order to drive the people away from the deen of Allāh and His Messenger.[37]

Imām Muhammad ibn 'AbdulWahhāb stated to Ismā'īl al-Jara'ī of Yemen:

As for the assertion that we hold the (Muslim) people in general to be disbelievers, it is a false allegation made public by the enemies to drive people away from this deen. We can only emphatically say that this is a naked lie![38]

Rasheed Ridā stated:

The books of the Shaykh contain what is contrary to the allegations. These books tell us that they do not pass the verdict of disbelief except against those who commit acts that are acts of disbelief according to the consensus of the Muslims.[39]

Imām Muhammad ibn 'AbdulWahhāb (rahimahullāh) also stated:

In regards to what has been said of me, that I make takfeer on the general body of Muslims then this a slander of the enemies, as well as their saying that I say whoever adheres to the Religion of Allāh and His Messenger while living in another land then it will not suffice him until he comes to me first then this also is a false accusation. Rather adherence to the Religion of Allāh and His Messenger is done in any land, however we do make takfeer of the one who affirms belief in the Religion of Allāh and His Messenger then turns away from it and diverts the people from it, likewise whoever worships idols after knowing that it is the religion of the Polytheists and a form of beautification to the common people, then this is what we make takfeer of as does every scholar on the face of the earth, they make takfeer of these people, except for the stubborn or ignorant person and Allāh knows best, Wa Salām.[40]

As for the sanctimonious references to the Ottoman Empire and that it ended in 1924 then this simplistic assertion has to be debunked. The reality is that the Ottoman state was already in a state of decline and stagnation by the nineteenth century, indeed by the eighteenth century, the factors of which would necessitate *al-Muhajiroun* and *Hizb ut-Tahreer* to make *takfeer* of it if it was in existence today, according to their rules. In the sixteenth and seventeenth centuries the capitulations system circumvented the independence of the Ottoman state. It was a system which meant that European traders living in Ottoman territory were not required to observe the law of the land and thus had their own courts and laws by which they were ruled by, they were no longer subject to government control. They were also not subject to taxes and could import and sell goods at any price they chose. Was this an example of a Prophetic Khilāfah according to *al-Muhajiroun* and *Hizb ut-Tahreer*?

By the last quarter of the eighteenth century, the gap between the technical skills of some Western and Northern European countries and those of the rest of the world grew wider and the Ottomans were left lagging. Was this an example of a Prophetic Khilāfah according to *al-Muhajiroun*? In 1791 CE the Ottomans could not sufficiently defend their territories to the extent that the British Prime Minister of the day, William Pitt, contemplated sending British troops to help the Sultan against the Czar of Russia during the Ottoman-Russian war.[41] Was this an example of a Prophetic Khilāfah according to *al-Muhajiroun* and *Hizb ut-Tahreer*? In 1838 during the Second Turko-Egyptian War, the German Field Marshall, head of the Prussian Army and military strategist Helmuth von Moltke the Elder, was requested by the Ottoman Sultan at the time Mahmūd the Second to

37

modernise the Ottoman army and advise Ottoman generals in their fight against Muhammad Ali Pasha.[42] Lieutenant Laue of Prussia was also requested. Muhammad Ali Pasha had rebelled in Egypt in 1831 in order to increase his control over Palestine, Syria and Arabia. Moltke published some of the letters he had written during that time as *Letters on Conditions and Events in Turkey in the Years 1835 to 1839*. Nicolas the First of Russia had also sent an army to aid the Ottomans against Muhammad Ali Pasha before in 1832 during the First Turko-Egyptian War. So non-Muslim military strategists and troops were used to fight against other Muslims:

Prussian advisors were viewed as the least suspect; and Helmuth von Moltke along with several others, aided Mahmud II from 1833-1839.[43]

Was this an example of a Prophetic Khilāfah according to *al-Muhajiroun* and *Hizb ut-Tahreer*? During the Crimean War (1854-1856)[44] the Ottomans had to seek the help of Britain and France against the Russians, was this an example of a Prophetic Khilāfah according to *al-Muhajiroun* and *Hizb ut-Tahreer*? The Ottoman state was in such a state in the nineteenth century that the European powers of France[45], Russia and Britain were occupying parts of its territory and various Ottoman provinces were semi-autonomous and under effective control of local rulers.[46] Was this an example of a Prophetic Khilāfah according to *al-Muhajiroun* and *Hizb ut-Tahreer*?

The *Tanzimat (Tandhīmāt)* reform era (1839-1876) brought with it a range of reforms such as the development of a secular school system, the introduction of new codes of commercial and criminal law based on French law and the abolition of the Jizya. Was this an example of a Prophetic Khilāfah according to *al-Muhajiroun* and *Hizb ut-Tahreer*? Lubna A. Alam states in a paper entitled *Keeping the State Out: The Separation of Law and State in Classical Islamic Law* that:

> The Ottoman Empire, on the other hand, enacted a fifteen-year statute of limitations on all crimes, including *qadhf*. This seemingly minor difference between classical Islamic doctrine and actual Ottoman practice exposes the wide shift that occurred in Islamic law during the Ottoman period. **The Ottomans' changes to the practice of Islamic law put them outside the classical era of Islamic law,** and "in the minds of most Muslims the Ottomans are simply not sufficiently representative of the classical tradition..."[47]

The Ottoman Penal Code of 1858 was based on the Napoleonic Code of 1810 and put aside Islamic punishments. It established a French-type court system with tribunals, courts of appeal and a high court of appeal all based on the hierarchy of the secular court system. This secular criminal code and court system remained until 1923.[48] Was this an example of a Prophetic Khilāfah according to al-Muhajiroun and Hizb ut-Tahreer?

Under the Ottoman Sultān 'AbdulHameed the Second (1876-1909) a new constitution called the 'Kanūn-i Esāsī' (Qānūn al-Asāsī) was established. The Constitution proposed a parliament divided into two parts: The senators were elected by the Sultān, and the Chamber of Deputies was elected by the people, although not directly (they chose delegates who would then choose the Deputies). There were also elections held every 4 years to keep the parliament changing and to continually express the voice of the people. Was this an example of a Prophetic Khilāfah according to al-Muhajiroun and Hizb ut-Tahreer?

The Ottoman Constitution on 1876 states under 'Chamber of Deputies': **"Article 66. The election is held by secret ballot. The mode of election will be determined by a special law"** and under 'Law Courts' says: **"Article 87. Affairs touching the Şeriat (i.e. Sharee'ah) are tried by the tribunals of the Şeriat. The judgment of civil affairs appertains to the civil tribunals"**[49] hereby differentiating between the Sharee'ah and Civil Law. Was this an example of a Prophetic Khilāfah according to al-Muhajiroun and Hizb ut-Tahreer? A secular law school, the Istanbul Law Faculty, was established in 1875 to train judges, advocates and public prosecutors for the non-Islamic courts.[50] Was this an example of a Prophetic Khilāfah according to al-Muhajiroun and Hizb ut-Tahreer?

The Ottomans had a state policy towards Arabic which was strong and institutionalized but then weakened, creating a barrier between most Muslims and the sources of Islām. Due to this, a whole host of religious innovations, invented 'spiritual' exercises and odd customs flourished along with blind following of madhhabs. Was this an example of a Prophetic Khilāfah according to al-Muhajiroun and Hizb ut-Tahreer? Allāh says,

$$﴿وَإِن تَتَوَلَّوْا يَسْتَبْدِلْ قَوْمًا غَيْرَكُمْ ثُمَّ لَا يَكُونُوا أَمْثَالَكُمْ﴾$$

"And if you turn away (i.e. refuse), He will replace you with another people; then they will not be the likes of you."
{Muhammad (47): 38}

Allāh also says, in another beautiful verse which shows Allāh's wisdom:

﴿يَا أَيُّهَا الَّذِينَ آمَنُوا مَن يَرْتَدَّ مِنكُمْ عَن دِينِهِ فَسَوْفَ يَأْتِي اللّهُ بِقَوْمٍ يُحِبُّهُمْ وَيُحِبُّونَهُ أَذِلَّةٍ عَلَى الْمُؤْمِنِينَ أَعِزَّةٍ عَلَى الْكَافِرِينَ يُجَاهِدُونَ فِي سَبِيلِ اللّهِ وَلاَ يَخَافُونَ لَوْمَةَ لآئِمٍ ذَلِكَ فَضْلُ اللّهِ يُؤْتِيهِ مَن يَشَاء وَاللّهُ وَاسِعٌ عَلِيمٌ﴾

"O you who have believed, whoever of you should revert from his religion – Allāh will bring forth (in place of them) a people He will love and who will love Him (who are) humble toward the believers, powerful against the disbelievers; they strive in the cause of Allāh and do not fear the blame of a critic. That is the favor of Allāh; He bestows it upon whom He wills. And Allāh is all-Encompassing and Knowing."
{al-Mā'idah (5): 54}

So what is the true driving force behind their need to perpetuate the myth of the Khilāfah system being dismantled in the year 1924? Why the need to cling to a fabricated belief - in spite of various authentic narrations and historical records recording the demise of the Khilāfah? Again this is just another point, to add to the many, which highlight their warped fascination with anything pertaining to rulership and governing. All members of *al-Muhajiroun* therefore fall into one of two types:

1. The blind-follower – this is the majority- who knows little about recorded history or prophetic narrations chronicling the demise and rejuvenation of the Khilāfah.
2. Those who are fully aware that the Khilāfah was dismantled centuries ago, but are willing to advocate a historical fallacy as the *de facto* standard in order to maintain their agenda.

Concerning the first group, there is not much to comment because they are basically juvenile *Muqallidūn* (Blind-followers). Most of them have only recently been liberated, either from a life of *jāhiliyah* or a strict regime of Blind-following one of the *Madhāhib*. Hopefully many of them will mature and eventually recognise the falsehood they have adopted for truth. As for the second group, who are fully aware that the Khilāfah never ended in 1924, their promotion of this myth is not so innocent or gullible. We believe the goal is to falsely instil in the Muslims that Islām, in the early 1920's, was a fully functioning system. Why the need? Perhaps it would aid their goals to convince the Muslims that it wasn't that long ago when the Muslims were ruling by the *Sharee'ah*. This could encourage the Muslims to subscribe to al-Muhājiroun's fast-track methods of rejuvenating Islām through the use of coups and other revolutionary tactics. When we confronted Anjem Choudhary and his followers regarding the "1924 Khilāfah/Sharee'ah" myth of the Ottoman Empire, in front of witnesses in Brixton on Saturday 25th April 2009, they were rendered speechless; for there is no debate when it comes to historical facts.

From an image association perspective, when we think of *al-Muhajiroun*, we think of young animated males parading the streets performing demonstrations and political rallies. For many this is the initial image which is conjured up after hearing or seeing the word 'al-Muhajiroun'. For most Muslims, the term 'Muhajiroun' used to be instantly related to our pious forefathers, those who left the abode of *kufr* at the time (Makkah) and migrated to the land of Islām (Madeenah). How many non-Muslims have even an inkling of what this name truly means? Most non-Muslims only know this name to be a title for a motley crew of misguided young men who love to parade themselves around the country by way of demonstrations and rallies while ranting and raving. This means that many Muslims and non-Muslims have begun to believe that demonstrations and rallies are a part of Islām. However, the reality is the opposite and the sobering truth is that such practises have no roots in Islām. In fact, many will argue that demonstrations and rallies are a by-product of Capitalism, Democracy and fringe politics. Some will even argue further and say such activities are nothing but democratic play-grounds manufactured to maintain the illusion of so-called "true democracy", which permits the masses to vent their anger and dismay without causing any real change (think Irāq war protests for example). Regardless of their purpose and origins, the fact is they have no legislated authority in Islām – actually any close scrutiny of the anatomy of demonstrations and one could easily say they are an unguarded door which enters into the realms of *khurūj* (revolution).

So what evidences does *al-Muhajiroun* provide to keep their well-oiled demonstration machine moving? The only "evidence" used by *al-Muhajiroun* for demonstrations is the story of 'Umar ibn al-Khattāb's conversion to Islām, in which the companions were organised into two lines, led by 'Umar and Hamza *(radi Allāhu 'anhum)*. They supposedly "marched" to the Ka'bah "demonstrating". This is their main proof, one of the *al-Muhajiroun* cult, namely the ignoramus "Abū Turāb" (aka 'AbdulQādir), mentions it in this video: http://www.youtube.com/watch?v=R2JbsTMj0Yw&feature=related See 50 seconds onwards. The hadeeth which mentions the incident is *da'eef*, Dr. 'Abdul'Azeez al-Fareeh said in his edit and checking of *Mahdus-Sawāb fī Fadā'il Ameeril-Mu'mineen Umar bin al-Khattāb*, vol.1, p.149 by Ibn ul-Mabrid (d.909AH):

> Recorded by Ibn ul-Jawzī in *al-Manāqib* (p.12), Reported by Abū Nu'aym in *ad-Dalaa'il* (vol.1, p.241), and in *al-Hilyah* (vol.1, p.40) and in its *isnad* is Ishāq bin Abī Farwah and he is Matrook (see *at-Taqreeb*, p.102). Also see *al-Isābah* of Ibnu Hajr (vol.4, p.280).

THE GRADUAL EVOLUTION OF OMAR BAKRĪ'S BELIEFS AND METHODOLOGY ALONG WITH THAT OF HIS FOLLOWERS

Omar Bakrī Muhammad Fustuq is a Syrian of dubious background and his name 'Fustuq', sometimes spelt 'Fostok', is the Arabic word for 'Pistachio nut' in Shām (Jordan, Palestine, Syria and Lebanon). According to the Islāmic researcher 'AbdurRahmān ibn Muhammad ad-Dimishqiyyah Omar Bakrī is: from Halab (Aleppo) and is Lebanese by residence (before and after his time in the UK). He was one of the main symbols of *Hizb ut-Tahreer* in the 1990s despite his ignorance of the Arabic language in general and of the Qur'ān specifically, in terms of reading, understanding and application;[51] not to mention his hastiness in delivering *'fatāwā'*! Bakrī is a pseudo scholar and a person of false propaganda and proof of this is that he claims in his book *Essential Fiqh* (London: Islāmic Book Company, 1996) that he graduated from numerous universities, the most of important of which being *Umm ul-Qura'* in Makkah, the *Islāmic University of Madeenah* and *al-Azhar* in Egypt, along with the *College of Sharee'ah* in Damascus!!? As he knew how honoured the names of Makkah and Madeenah were with the non-Arab Muslims, he claimed that he spent his life studying between these two holy cities.

A classical example of the evil effects of incorrect *da'wah* which opposes the Divine Prophetic methodology can be seen in unfortunate incidents which arise in the household. Sordid expositions of the antics of family members clarify the emptiness and ineptitude of the efforts of the likes of Bakrī in the field of enjoining the good and forbidding the evil; and he is regarded as being a "Shaykh", "leader" and "Islāmic preacher". So how on earth can one embark on a crusade to enjoin the good and forbid the evil on the whole Muslim world, when the manifest evils which plague one's own home are forsaken? So priority is given to rectifying the whole world over one's family members? Did not Allāh remind us in His Book:

﴾يَا أَيُّهَا الَّذِينَ ءَامَنُوا قُوا أَنفُسَكُمْ وَأَهْلِيكُمْ نَاراً وَقُودُهَا النَّاسُ وَالْحِجَارَةُ﴿

"O you who have believed, protect yourselves and your families from a Fire whose fuel is people and stones..."
{Tahreem (66): 6}

Ibn Katheer *(rahimahullāh)* stated in his *tafseer* of this *ayah*:
"Protect yourselves and your families from a Fire (Hell)..." saying, "Have taqwa of Allāh and order your family to have taqwa of Him." Qatādah said, "He commands obedience to Allāh, to not disobey Allāh, he orders his family to obey His orders and helps them to act upon His orders. When one sees disobedience, he stops them and forbids them from doing it." Similar was said by ad-Dahhāk and Muqātil; "It is an obligation for the Muslim to teach his near family members, and his male and female slaves what Allāh has made obligatory for them and what Allāh has forbidden for them." There is a hadith that confirms the meaning of this Ayah. Ahmad, Aboo Dawud and at-Tirmidhee recorded that ar-Rabi' bin Sabrah said that his father said that the Messenger of Allāh said: "Protect yourselves and your families from a Fire (Hell)..." He said, "Work in the obedience of Allāh, avoid disobedience of Allāh and order your families to remember Allāh, then Allāh will save you from the Fire."

Therefore, the blatant obstinacy and rejection which may be witnessed from members of the household may partly be a symptom of the type of Islām which is taught in the home. Thus, if you are exposed to a militant, deviant form of Islām, then this may have an adverse effect on the children, and very well cause them to reject Islām, not only in speech, but also in action. If anything this is a timely and much needed reminder of where rectification of our wayward Ummah must truly begin. Abū Hurayrah *(radi Allāh 'anhu)* narrated that the Prophet *(sallallāhu 'alayhi wassallam)* said: *"Each of you is a shepherd and each of you is responsible for his flock."*[52] The word 'his' being the operative word here, since it is well known that rectification starts at home. How can a man observe and rectify the problems of other people's flocks when his own flock has the devoted attention of the wolf?

In a Channel 4 documentary in 1996 entitled 'The Tottenham Ayatollah', which Omar Bakrī freely and mutually participated in, as did Anjem Choudhary, Abu Izzaddeen and others, it was highlighted that he lived in a council house on income support while applying for a British passport!? Indeed even the producer of the documentary, who is of Jewish background, stated that he found Bakrī "clownish". Are these characteristics from the hallmarks which embellish the people of knowledge? The documentary was also placed on the 'Islāmbase.co.uk' website which is a site run by some individuals linked to followers of Omar Bakrī, but recently they have removed it! We refer to those affiliated to Omar Bakrī as "cult followers" as all the features of cultish behaviour are observable, most particularly in the following fundamental cult traits:

- ✓ Uncritical following of a leader and acceptance of all that he says with little or no question
- ✓ A leader who has control over the followers by claiming to be on a true mission.
- ✓ Involvement in illegal activities (related to incitement)
- ✓ Violent rhetoric, sometimes in order to attract attention and build up the rapport and fame of the cult.
- ✓ Publicity stunts
- ✓ Deceptive tactics utilised in the recruitment of followers, this is linked to the Islāmic idea of tadlees, which will be discussed later in the study.
- ✓ Simplistic indoctrination via reference to contorting texts.
- ✓ Restricting understanding of the texts.
- ✓ Accumulation of wealth for personal and political aims.
- ✓ Providing simplistic quick-fix solutions to deep-rooted problems.
- ✓ Whatever the dubious leader dictates goes, whether these are rules, regulations or so forth.
- ✓ A leader who knows full well that what is being taught is false yet has to maintain control.
- ✓ Members give the cult leadership wealth in order to further the religio-political aims of the group.

In the mid 1990s Omar Bakrī Muhammad Fustuq was the main head of Hizb ut-Tahreer in the UK, then after a split he left them and set up al-Muhajiroun. More recently (from around 2002) Bakrī's cult began to acknowledge a very restricted understanding of *tawheed* due to the constant emphasis which the Salafis placed on it during mutual discussion. Before we discuss the reasons which have led Omar Bakrī and his followers to now don the gowns of the Sunnah and *Salafiyyah* it is important to highlight that such re-grouping, splitting, changing and instability are all the hallmarks of *Ahl ul-Bida'* (people of religious innovation). Allāh says,

﴿وَلاَ تَكُونُواْ كَالَّذِينَ تَفَرَّقُواْ وَاخْتَلَفُواْ مِن بَعْدِ مَا جَآءَهُمُ الْبَيِّنَاتُ وَأُوْلَـئِكَ لَهُمْ عَذَابٌ عَظِيمٌ﴾

"And do not be like the ones who became divided and differed after the clear proofs had come to them. And those will have a great punishment."

{Āli 'Imrān (3): 105}

And Allāh says,

﴿وَلاَ تَكُونُواْ مِنَ الْمُشْرِكِينَ – مِنَ الَّذِينَ فَرَّقُواْ دِينَهُمْ وَكَانُواْ شِيَعاً كُلُّ حِزْبٍ بِمَا لَدَيْهِمْ فَرِحُونَ﴾

"...and do not be of those who associate others with Allāh, [or] of those who have divided their religion and become sects, every faction rejoicing in what it has."

{ar-Room (30): 31-32}

And Allāh says,

﴿إِنَّ الَّذِينَ فَرَّقُواْ دِينَهُمْ وَكَانُواْ شِيَعًا لَّسْتَ مِنْهُمْ فِى شَىْءٍ﴾

"Indeed, those who have divided their religion and become sects – you, [O Muhammad], are not [associated] with them in anything."

{al-An'ām (6): 159}

Imām ash-Shātibī *(rahimahullāh)* states in his monumental work on *bida', al-I'tisām,* that the above *ayah* has been understood by the *Mufassireen* as being applicable to *Ahl ul-Bida'*.[53] Indeed, Imām ash-Shātibī highlights that one of the causes for splitting and division is:

«أن يعتقد الإنسان في نفسه أو يُعْتَقَدَ فيه أنه من أهل العلم والاجتهاد في الدين،

ولم يبلغ تلك الدرجة»

"When a person believes, or others believe that the person, is from the people of 'Ilm (knowledge) and ijtihād in the deen when in fact the person has not reached that level whatsoever."[54]

The following story illustrates this:

قال: مالك بن أنس:(بكى ربيعة يوماً بكاء شديداً، فقيل له: مصيبة نزلت بك؟

فقال: لا ولكن استفتي من لا علم عنده!)

Imām Mālik bin Anas (rahimahullāh) said: "One day Rabee'ah was crying immensely, so he was asked 'has a calamity befallen you?' Rabee'ah replied: 'No! But a person without knowledge was asked to give a fatwa.'"[55]

This is relevant as *Hizb ut-Tahreer* in the UK in the mid-1990s were the ones who set Omar Bakrī up as being a "Mufti", yet it is important to know that giving *fatāwā* is not for every Tom, Dick and Bakrī! *Al-Muhajiroun* would later proclaim Bakrī as a "Mujtahid Murajjih" (!?).[56] Let's have a brief look at the conditions for *ijtihād*, as highlighted by Imām Muhammad bin Sālih al-'Uthaymeen (rahimahullāh) in al-Usūl min 'Ilm il-Usūl:

شروط الاجتهاد:

للاجتهاد شروط منها:

– أن يعلم من الأدلة الشرعية ما يحتاج إليه في اجتهاده كآيات الأحكام وأحاديثها.

– أن يعرف ما يتعلق بصحة الحديث وضعفه؛ كمعرفة الإسناد ورجاله، وغير ذلك.

– أن يعرف الناسخ والمنسوخ ومواقع الإجماع حتى لا يحكم بمنسوخ أو مخالف للإجماع،!

- أن يعرف من الأدلة ما يختلف به الحكم من تخصيص، أو تقييد، أو نحوه حتى لا يحكم بما يخالف ذلك.

- أن يعرف من اللغة وأصول الفقه ما يتعلق بدلالات الألفاظ؛ كالعام والخاص والمطلق والمقيد والمجمل والمبين، ونحو ذلك؛ ليحكم بما تقتضيه تلك الدلالات.

- أن يكون عنده قدرة يتمكن بها من استنباط الأحكام من أدلتها.

The conditions for ijtihād include:

1. That he knows the Divinely Legislated evidences that are needed in his *ijtihād*, such as the *āyāt* of *ahkām* (regulations) and the *ahādeeth*.

2. That he knows the authentic and the inauthentic *ahādeeth*, like understanding the chains of transmission, the narrators and whatever else in this regard.

3. That he knows the abrogated and the unabrogated verses along with the instances of *ijmā'* (consensus) so that he does not rule with that which is abrogated or oppose the consensus.

4. That he knows from the evidences variant rulings based on *takhsees* (specification) or *taqyeed* (restriction) or the likes. This is so that he does not issue a ruling which is contrary to this.

5. That he knows from the Arabic language and *Usūl ul-Fiqh* that which is connected to what textual implications. Such as: the general ('*ām*) and the specific (*khās*), the absolute (*mutlaq*) and the restricted (*muqayyid*), the general and ambivalent (*mujmal*) and explicit (*mubeen*) – in order to give a ruling based on what these implications depend upon.

6. That he has the ability with which to make *istinbāt* (deriving and extracting rulings) of the regulations from its evidences.

For more on the conditions that have to be maintained for *ijtihād* refer to Imām ash-Shāfi'ī's *Risālah*, pp.509-511;[57] *Ibtāl ul-Istihsān*, p.40;[58] Ibn 'AbdulBarr, *Jāmi' Bayān ul-'Ilm wa Fadlihi*, vol.2, p.61;[59] Ibn Qudāmah al-Maqdisī, *Rawdat un-Nādhir*, vol.2, pp.401-406;[60] Shaykh ul-Islām Ibn Taymiyyah, *Majmū' al-Fatāwā*, vol.20, p.583;[61] Ibn ul-Qayyim, *I'lām ul-Muwaqqi'een*, vol.1, p.46;[62] *Sharh ul-Kawkab il-Muneer*, vol.4, pp.459-467;[63]

ash-Shinqītī's *Mudhakkirat Usūl ul-Fiqh*, pp.311-312.[64] There are a whole host of issues related to the conditions of *ijtihād*, some of which will be mentioned later, and the conditions of a *Mufti* and his manners and characteristics which could also be mentioned.[65] What is noticeable, that at the very least, it is questionable whether Omar Bakrī Muhammad has fulfilled any of these conditions, and this study will indeed demonstrate why this is the case.

Due to the constant pressure that the Salafis placed on this *hizb* regarding the importance of calling to *tawheed*, this ultimately caused them to succumb to the primary obligation of calling to *tawheed*. However, still hell-bent on maintaining their political objectives they adopted an innovated concept of *tawheed* and its categories, which opposed the classical definition.[66] Thus, in their rhetoric related to *tawheed* it can be observed that in most cases they give reference to *'al-Hākimiyyah'* (rulership and 'sovereignty'), which in itself is not a category in and of itself, rather an aspect of one of the main categories. Which may provoke the question, why the need to extract a part of *tawheed* which is found in one of its main categories, and then promote it as one of its main categories? Their current talks and lectures therefore prove this point clearly, as can be seen in some of the lectures on *tawheed* that are available from the internet. Seeing the opportunity which lies within the force of *tawheed*, they cunningly recognised the political potential this term and concept has in recruiting the youth and the masses, cue their constant referral to the innovated category of *Tawheed ul-Hākimiyyah* and rulership. Thinking that by limiting *tawheed* to the misguidance of the Muslim leaders, this will somehow solve our woeful predicaments. Their adoption of *tawheed* therefore is nothing but a superficial one, as to appease Ahl us-Sunnah, the Salafis, and to give the false impression that they are calling to the truth, upon the truth, not forgetting, that it was actually the Salafis who initially placed pressure on them to give precedence and importance to *tawheed*.

So prior to this also, they never wore *thobes* or focused on the Sunnah, the documentary *Tottenham Ayatollah* is proof of this wherein Anjem Choudhary, Abū Izzaddeen and others can be seen with trimmed beards, *musbil (garments below their ankles)*, wearing suits and resembling those who

49

they never tire of reminding the Muslims about (i.e. the *Kuffār*) in attire and appearance[67] and up until 2002 they only discussed:

✓ *Khilāfah*
✓ *Politics*
✓ *Removing the rulers, after making takfeer of the Muslim ones of them*
✓ *Khabr ul-Āhād should not be taken into 'aqeedah*
✓ *Allegiance to the kuffār*

Therefore, the current political activities of Bakrī's groups are due to their *Hizb ut-Tahreer* origins, but Bakrī and his fraternity split from *Hizb ut-Tahreer* over the issue of where exactly the Khilāfah is to be established, Bakrī and his followers holding that it could be established in the UK!? As for Omar Bakrī being "Salafi" then this is absolutely false, and his extreme and outrageous statements are the best testimony to that, as we have seen straight from the horse's filthy mouth (as it were!).

The very fact that the movements and organisations of Omar Bakrī and his blind followers have undergone such metamorphosis indicates that they have no solid foundation or basis. For if they are truly upon the correct way, then why do they have to change every year or two?! So they emulate the Salafis only in matters which do not conflict or compromise their own political-Khawārij agenda, trying to emulate the *da'wah Salafiyyah* in many ways like a wolf in sheep's clothing. So they recognise what amounts to the truth but still stubbornly follow their desires, hence their adoption of the name "Salafi" and falsely calling to *tawheed* (when they only emphasise Hākimiyyah). The phenomenon observed in their compulsive, ritual name changing is the clearest example of their misguidance and falsehood. So what is the catalyst for such erratic behaviour? Does the truth need to conform, adapt and change like this? When medicated over, what becomes apparent is that such idiosyncrasy is actually a sign of falsehood – as it is falsehood alone that feels the need to evolve and adapt - ever trying to mimic the truth and go with the flow of the zeitgeist. But what is important to note here is the important Arabic saying which is replete in the writings of the Islāmic scholars that:

$$\text{«لسان الحال أبين من لسان المقال»}$$

A person's condition is clearer than verbal expression

(Or as is said with the English expression: 'actions speak louder than words')
Or with the use of different elatives *(asmā ut-tafdeel)* such as:

«لسان الحال أصدق من لسان المقال»

Or:

«لسان الحال أبلغ من لسان المقال»

Or:

«لسان الحال أفصح من لسان المقال»

Or:

«لسان الحال أقوى من لسان المقال»

Another principle that if oft-repeated within the books of *Usūl* is:

«العبرة بالحقائق والمعاني لا بالألفاظ والمباني»

"What are important are the realities and the meanings (that are applied), not terms and structures"

(so if there is a contradiction between a term and the reality of what is being manifest then the reality and what it means is what is of importance, despite the use of a mere term)

Another principle found in the books of *Usūl* is:

«ادعاء المُسميات لا يُلزم ثبوت الصفات»

"Claiming names does not necessitate affirmation of the characteristics (of those names)"

These profound expressions and principles are going to be primary for this study, for they indicate that despite what a person says, his true condition is always shown by his actions. Therefore, despite bold claims to *Salafiyyah* and sayings and slogans about following the Salafi *manhaj*, these slogans mean nothing when one's true condition and actions can tell us more as to whether a person is truly and sincerely following the correct Salafi understanding or not. Within the *Usūl* of Ahl us-Sunnah is the fact that:

The main example (to follow) is the way of the Ahl ul-Hadeeth and their manhaj, so whoever says with his tongue "I am from Ahl ul-Hadeeth" and may have even studied hadeeth then he is not considered to be from the Ahl ul-Hadeeth until he traverses their way and manhaj, so what is of importance is that a person's condition is more indicative than verbal expression (actions speak louder than words).[68]

Indeed, of the characteristics of the *Ahl ul-Bida'* (people of innovation) is that they formulate false principles and then scavenge the sources to justify such principles and give them credence. So *Ahl ul-Bida'* take something from Islām which is sound and then stealthily annex to it a principle of *bāṭil* (falsehood). Imām Muhammad bin Sālih al-'Uthaymeen *(rahimahullāh)* stated in his commentary on *at-Tahdheer min Fitnat it-Takfeer*, pp.68-69:

> Another matter is that can be appended to that is: evil intent necessitates evil understanding, because when a person wants and intends something this necessitates a person transmitting his understanding in accordance to what he wants and intends, and then he distorts the texts accordingly. From the well-known principles of the 'Ulama was that they used to say: deduce then believe, don't believe and then deduce and be misguided. The three reasons are:
> 1 – Lack of Shari' knowledge.
> 2 – Lack of fiqh of Shari' principles
> 3 – Evil understanding resulting from evil intent and desire.

Due to the infatuation with politics that the cults of Omar Bakrī Muhammad have had over the many years, they have not taken the time out to establish a place of *'ibādah* in the city of Luton for example as they have been banned from many of the *masājid* in the city due to their extremism and reliance on sensationalism to increase their circulation. Furthermore, they have total dependence and reliability upon one man, that being Omar Bakrī Muhammad, who they have to run to in most matters, in many ways similar to the workings of a cult. There are few other sources of Islāmic knowledge that they refer to other than dubious Bakrī and this in itself is contrary to the *deen* and correct methodology. This partisan *taqleed* in itself is a clear indication that they are not Salafi in their outlook, methodology and belief.

CLAIMING BROAD SUPPORT FROM THE MUSLIM COMMUNITY VIA INVENTING NEW ORGANISATIONS

A main characteristic of the cults of Omar Bakri is that they manufacture pseudonyms for organisations to give over the impression that they are supported, by and large, by a broad range of organisations within the Muslim community. So not only does their dynamic name-changing occur for political reasons but also to fabricate mass support of their da'wah. Therefore, we find with Bakri's followers that they have made up the following organisations, which do not actually exist as separate organisations as they claim:

- ✓ *Concerned Muslims for Justice*
- ✓ *Luton Dawah Project*
- ✓ *Global Shariah Society*
- ✓ *Movement for Shariah in the UK*
- ✓ *Muslims Against Freedom and Democracy*
- ✓ *Society of Muslim Parents*
- ✓ *Islamic Media Monitoring Forum*
- ✓ *International Islamic Front* and
- ✓ *Society of Converts to Islam*

This underlines the deceptive nature of the cult and its willingness to claim any amount of information in order to gain support from Muslims. The famous Machiavellian principle raises it head again: "the ends justify the means". Their Chameleon like-ways which cause them to adapt when their environment is threatened, have taken form all under the guise of the following names mainly:

1. AL-MUHAJIROUN: "THE VOICE, THE EYES, AND THE EARS"

This very name of this group defies intuition and remains a paradox as where did they actually make *hijrah* to? Many of them, if not most, are still residing in non-Muslim lands! This name was probably changed as it did not reflect an atom of truth of their teachings and practices. This begs the question, why did they designate the title 'al-Muhājiroon' for themselves? In Islāmic history did not the historical *Muhājiroon* (emigrants) show their disgust against *kufr* by actually leaving the abode of *kufr*? Why do we witness the exact opposite from these people? One could even challenge the claim that they hate the *kuffār* as much as they would like us to believe, in fact, their existence is inextricably linked to the political machinations of the *kuffār* along with paying concern to the zeitgeist with reference to the Muslims.

This phase also witnessed the rise of the likes of Anjem Choudhary (a London solicitor who has become Bakrī's deputy), Abū 'Izzadeen 'Umar Brooks, 'AbdurRahmān Saleem and others from East London and Luton (such as Abū Farooq and others). The use of luminous-coloured stickers and posters, ranting and raving, publicity stunts, rabble-rousing and opposing the Prophetic mannerisms in giving *da'wah* all characterised this phase, as the group became a contorted version and continuation of the *Hizb ut-Tahreer UK* of the mid-1990s. So the vociferous, noisy, screaming-in-the-streets *da'wah* with which Omar Bakrī Muhammad made *Hizb ut-Tahreer UK* achieve notoriety in the mid-1990s, was continued over into Bakrī's new partisan group *al-Muhajiroun*. There was also emphasis on simplistic slogans, again carried over from *Hizb ut-Tahreer UK* under Bakrī, wherein statements which emphasised quick-fix **"solutions"** to various **"systems"** were regurgitated.

Another interesting member of *al-Muhajiroun* during this period was one individual who has recently attempted to present himself as a "reformed Islāmist-extremist" in order to gain attention, secure lucrative book deals and win the ear of the media and certain UK government officials. However, there are serious discrepancies in many of his claims and he may have even fabricated some of his stories. In this way, he resembles another individual, who incidentally was also an ex-Omar Bakrī groupie! Therefore, we can see the constant shape-shifting and political antics of those associated with Omar Bakrī, which they in fact inherited from him, and the extreme polarities which they go to without remaining on the balanced course. Allāh says,

$$﴿وَكَذَٰلِكَ جَعَلْنَـٰكُمْ أُمَّةً وَسَطًا لِّتَكُونُوا۟ شُهَدَآءَ عَلَى النَّاسِ وَيَكُونَ الرَّسُولُ عَلَيْكُمْ شَهِيدًا﴾$$

"And thus we have made you a just community that you will be witnesses over the people and the Messenger will be a witness over you."
{Baqarah (2): 143}

54

Muslim and Abū Dāwood record that Ibn Mas'ood *(radi Allāhu 'anhu)* narrated that the Prophet *(sallallāhu 'alayhi wassallam)* stated: *"The extremists are destroyed, the extremists are destroyed, the extremists are destroyed."* The fact that the Prophet *(sallallāhu 'alayhi wassallam)* stated it three times indicates the emphasis on this.

Al-Muhajiroun officially disbanded in 2004 CE based on the instruction of Omar Bakrī Muhammad. Former members and defectors include one individual who is currently a Public Speaker and philosophy student at *Birkbeck University* in London who was a *al-Muhajiroun* member and then left the group several years before they officially disbanded.[69] However, many of the former cult members, even though they have rejected much of Omar Bakrī's methods, have still have retained aspects of the teaching of Omar Bakrī Muhammad, and in the case of one ex-*al-Muhajiroun* follower for example that will be seen in point number 7 in the list of major differences between Salafis and the cult followers of Omar Bakrī.

Furthermore, the followers of Bakrī began using the name 'al-Muhajiroun' again in East London in March 2009 as they posted up the old posters again in East London in anticipation of publicity for their planned protests in Luton later on in that month. On their website 'Islam4UK.com', on Thursday 28 May 2009, they declared – which ended with an exclamation mark as if it's a wonderful thing - that the name 'al-Muhajiroun 'is to be re-launched'. They tell us:

Established in 1996, Al-Muhajiroun has long been regarded as one of the most influential Islamic organisations to have pierced the United Kingdom.

Swiftly moving around their obvious, self-pretentious declaration, exactly who else has regarded them to be one of the most 'influential Islamic organisations'? If our memories serve us correctly, was this not the same 'influential Islamic organisation' that was forced to put a sword to its own movement's name? Does changing your name due to public unrest and bad sentiments seem like a product of positive influence?! Such words as 'one of the most influential Islamic organisations', from an Islamic perspective, seem like words which are written *about* you rather than words you write about yourself. It is not uncommon for a complex to drive an individual to say such remarks, due to their need for self-convincement or hunger to convince others. Perhaps the correct three-worded phrase would be 'controversial Muslim organisation'. It was their controversial proclamations and public antics which provided them with such notoriety in the beginning. We would also like to add here that to merit the usage of the term 'Islamic' the first step would be to concur with Islām's teachings and not to variably oppose them. Then they go on to preposterously claim that:

...it also strived to confront the ills of society and invite the masses to the Deen of al-Islam as a complete way of life, and was extremely successful in doing so.

So we ask, where exactly have al-Muhajiroun been 'extremely successful'? The Richter scale for measuring the magnitude of their success could in theory be presented in three ways:

✓ Establishment of their main objective; that being an Islamic *Sharee'ah* system fully functional on the shores of the UK.

✓ Calling the masses to Islam through correct representation of Islām in matters of belief, practise and manners.

✓ Convincing the masses of Muslims that their brand of Islām is the same brand with which Allāh sent his Messenger *(sallallāhu 'alayhi wasallam)*.

As for possibility number one, then it is safe to say that they are nowhere remotely near to even establishing various masjids around Britain – let alone the inauguration of an Islamic State! Also, their aspirations and endeavours will never amount to anything until they sincerely repent, acknowledge the truth and adopt the Prophetic methodology for the establishment of Islam. The Divine formula for reviving Islam has been provided and explained. All we need to do is to adhere to the footsteps which were once trod by our illustrious forefathers.

Swiftly moving on to number two, have they accumulated any success in calling the masses to Islam through good conduct and kind gesture? During their time in the lime-light have they managed to convince large portions of the non-Muslims that their salvation only exists within the boundaries of Islam? Exactly how many converts have they added to their ranks? Besides conversions, what positive image have they sketched in the many minds of UK citizens regarding the beauty of Islam? Were placards held aloft in Luton that read "No Sharia Law" and chants such as "Terrorists Out" part of their plan for the implementation of Sharia law on

British soil? Was their success plan contingent on pushing many ignorant, non-Muslims to absurdly see some justice and logic in the far-right calls of the BNP? Was the rampaging of hundreds through the town of Luton, intimidating local people and attacking Asian residents a part of their success story too? How about the petrol bombing of a Luton based Mosque and Primary school, was this also a part of their success story? We think it would be relatively safe to conclude that al-Muhajiroun - due to their irresponsible and immature actions - have pushed many people's perceptions and thoughts of Islām right back to the Crusades.

So what about point three? Is there really wide, popular support for al-Muhajiroun? Based on the negative sentiments that circulate the Muslim communities in Luton and Brixton, we think not. Many notables in Luton gathered together for a meeting to curb the antics of al-Muhajiroun in anticipation of a foreseeable blowback. Alas, after the unfortunate incident which transpired at the Islamic centre in Luton, it was a little too late. The next paragraph makes some bold assertions:

> Following months of contemplation and research Sheikh Omar Bakri Muhammad, the former worldwide Ameer of Al-Muhajiroun, notably declared his change in aqeedah and subsequently Al-Muhajiroun also became a prominent front for the sect Ahlus Sunnah Wal Jama'ah, continuing to struggle in its confrontation against man-made law.

We found it interesting that the writers continually referred to Omar Bakri as "the former Ameer of al-Muhajiroun." One gets the impression here that gradual steps are being made in the opposite direction of Bakri. The latter part of this paragraph (once again) highlights their warped fascination with a single aspect of man's oppressive ways, against himself and others. Why so much energy directed towards the rulers and law-makers? And so little energy invested in the millions upon millions of Muslims who perform *shirk* in acts of worship with Allah every day? The declaration goes on:

> However, we would like to declare that after almost 15 years since the establishment of Al-Muhajiroun, and 5 years since its disbandment, Al-Muhajiroun is to be re-launched in the United Kingdom and to resume its activities as normal.

Here is the real deceptive part of their announcement. They declare here that al-Muhajiroun was disbanded 5 years ago, however such a claim couldn't be further from the truth. How would the claim stand under the scrutiny of a more simplistic scenario? Perhaps then we will see vividly the shallowness of their claim. If a man has the beliefs of the Shi'a, but decides one day to declare that he is no longer a member of the Shi'a, but despite this he still believes and practices everything which distinguishes the Shi'a, would his verbal dissociation be sufficient to free him from affiliation? No it wouldn't. Then the same logic must apply to al-Muhajiroun. And that is because every ingredient which made up al-Muhajiroun's beliefs, practises and persona did not cease to exist with the dissolving of their group's name. The formula of beliefs plus practises plus same old antics minus name, does not equate to the dismantling of al-Muhajiroun. It seems here that they are exploiting deceptive tactics employed by political organisations to dupe the masses into believing there has been a much needed change in the political arena.

What activity will they resume that they don't already participate in now? What dead belief or practise will they have to exhume in order to justify this dubious announcement? The tactic here is nothing more than to reiterate and consolidate the false notion that al-Muhajiroun, as a tangible entity, had once disbanded. However, the reality is that al-Muhajiroun has never disbanded. The aim was to publicly condemn their original pseudonym ("al-Muhajiroun") to exile due to public humiliation and also to avoid the possibility of being disbanded by law on account of public pressure. But as a physical, collective entity, they still remained at large, as it were, calling to the same innovated principles and performing the same immature antics which initially forced them to relinquish their group's name. The only real change was to adopt the title Ahlus Sunnah Wal Jama'ah to temporarily alleviate public hostility which was gathering momentum against them. We conclude with an interesting quote:

We would also like to stress particularly to the British public that Al-Muhajiroun is a completely legal organisation and hence the recommencement of its structure, activities and projects should be seen in this light.

They thus refer to being "legal", meaning by that being within in the confines of the man-made British law which they spend so much time telling us that they want to do away with. Why now the sudden acknowledgement of what is "legal" when they have never ever had any regard for it over the last ten years? Rather, unconditional, active contempt against man-made law has always been a pivotal part of their *da'wah*. Yet again, another indication of their chameleon-like transformations, this time however in the form of "going legit", as it were. Perhaps the energy they invest in worrying whether or not the British public perceive them as 'a legal organisation' would be better directed into trying to acquire the answer for the following question; does the law of Islām consider you as 'a completely legal organisation'?

2. THE "SAVED SECT"

Which the British government referred to as the *'Saviour Sect'*, which was good actually as at least they did not corrupt the original foundation of this name! The *'Firqat un-Nājiyyah'* mentioned in the hadeeth however is not a political party which changes every two years rather it is an ascription to the understanding of the correct path as exemplified by the Prophet Muhammad *(sallallāhu 'alayhi wassallam)* and his companions *(radi Allāhu 'anhum)*. The Prophet *(sallallāhu 'alayhi wassallam)* described the *Firqat un-Nājiyyah* as being *"What I and my companions are upon."*[70] Not as: "what I and Omar Bakrī Muhammad Fustuq are upon"! One of the recent Salafi Imāms, Imām 'Abdul'Azeez bin Bāz *(rahimahullāh)* stated:

> If there is a person or group which calls to the Book of Allāh and the Sunnah of His Messenger, and calls to the tawheed of Allāh and following of His Sharee'ah – then they are the Jama'ah and from the Firqat un-Nājiyyah. As for whoever calls to other than the Book of Allāh, and to other than the Sunnah of His Messenger – then such a person is not from the Jama'ah, rather he is from the misguided destroyed sects. As for the Firqat un-Nājiyyah then they are the preachers to the Book of Allāh and the Sunnah, even if there are groups of them here and there (around the world) as long as the goal and 'aqeedah is one.[71]

3. AL-GHURABĀ

Which is another *Shari'* produced name mentioned in the Sunnah which they used for their partisan political agenda. They used the name "al-Ghurabā" because perhaps somehow they emotionally indentified with this name due to the estranged position within which they found themselves due to their extreme political outlook. Not only an estranged position amongst the non-Muslims but also with regards to the Muslim community. Furthermore, the titles *'al-Ghurabā'* (the "Strangers") and *'Firqat un-Nājiyyah'* (the "Saved Sect") are not titles which one can officially name oneself with as part of a political group. It is one thing to refer to this title when explaining the characteristics of the people of the Sunnah "al-Ghurabā", but it's another thing to actually personify its title and you personify it due to your rigid adherence to the Sunnah. Ironically, we could agree that they are "ghurabā" in a linguistic sense, as they are "strange" in terms of their distance from Islām! But their isolated fringe beliefs and methodology give them no right to then exploit the term for their own neo-Khawārij political agenda. Their attempt to hijack the Islāmic usage of the terms "Saved Sect" and "al-Ghurabā" for their political gains, in order to seek sympathy from the Muslims, is nothing but an emotional plea which should fall on deaf ears. The very fact that they have abandoned these terms, after abusing them for their own deviated short-term objectives, proves that they had at best a superficial understanding of such profound, penetrating lofty titles. Their use of these two titles therefore was just as a temporary feel good factor.

4. THE "LONDON SCHOOL OF SHARIAH"

Another front name for Omar Bakrī's cult followers, changing name more times than a baby changes its nappies! This title however is to give over a sense of academia and scholarship to their neo-Khawārij political agenda. This is nothing but a sexed up name to present a more dignified appearance of this notorious group of cult followers of Omar Bakrī Muhammad. Do they really believe that names can somehow eradicate the realities which have and still do personify this group? This name represents nothing, but an apologetic cover up for all their past embarrassing events and publicity stunts.

As for the tangible substance of the "London School of Shariah" then where is the premises of this institution and what are the core curricula being taught? Surely if "students" are to enrol they would need to be able to see what is on offer.

5. "AHLUS SUNNAH WAL JAMĀ'AH"
Another *Shari'* title which they have attempted to hijack as an exclusive political party, they have used it in this political sense since November 2005 CE. At least a snake sheds its skin in one continuous piece, not so for this ever changing *hizb*!

6. "SALAFI YOUTH FOR ISLĀMIC PROPAGATION" (AND "SALAFI YOUTH ASSOCIATION" AND "SALAFI YOUTH MOVEMENT")
So could this title be considered the cumulative title dreamt about by *al-Muhajiroun*? Is this the hat which dons this 'evolutionary suit' change? Is this title the *crème de la crème*? This title has been in use since September 2008 CE and is the topic of this research, later we will table and chart the differences between Salafis and Omar Bakrī's cult followers who have begun to exploit the name "Salafi" as if it is another political Islāmic activist group. Al-'Allāmah Sālih al-Fawzān was asked:

"Is 'Salafiyyah' a hizb (partisan group)? Is ascription to it censured? Who are their scholars?"

Answer from al-'Allāmah Sālih al-Fawzān:

> Salafiyyah is the Firqat un-Nājiyyah and they are Ahl us-Sunnah wa'l-Jama'ah, Salafiyyah is not a hizb (party) from among the range of (political) parties which are named as such today. Salafiyyah is the Hizb of Allāh and His soldiers they are a Jama'ah upon the Sunnah and deen...Salafiyyah is: what the madhhab of the Salaf was upon and what the Messenger of Allāh (sallallāhu 'alayhi wassallam) and his companions were upon. It is not a party from among the range of contemporary (political) parties, rather it is an old Jama'ah from the time of the Messenger of Allāh (sallallāhu 'alayhi wassallam) and is hereditary and continuous, for they will not cease to be upon the truth manifest up until the hour is established, as the Prophet (sallallāhu 'alayhi wassallam) informed.[72]

Al-'Allāmah Sālih al-Fawzān was also asked:

"Some people claim that Salafiyyah is a group from among the other groups which are working throughout the world and so the ruling of it is like that of the other Islāmic groups. What are your observations regarding this claim?"

Answer from al-'Allāmah Fawzān:

What we mention is that the Jama'ah as-Salafiyyah is that which is upon the truth and has to be adhered to, co-operated with and ascribed to. It is not to be included with these (other) groups and it must not be considered as being among the opposing da'wah groups. How can we follow a sect which is contrary to the Jama'ah of Ahl us-Sunnah and the guidance of the Salaf us-Sālih? So the saying that "the Jama'ah of Salafiyyah is one of many other groups" is incorrect, as the Jama'ah of Salafiyyah is the original Jama'ah which has to be followed and its methodology traversed.[73]

Omar Bakrī since 2002 has claimed that he is from the people of Sunnah, yet he:

- ✓ Still has not openly admitted his error of "teaching" and supporting the *Shee'ah madhdhab* and claiming that it is from Islām. Indeed, in the mid-90s Bakrī was well known for praising al-Khomeini.

- ✓ Still has not accounted for why in his book entitled *Essential Fiqh* (London: The Islāmic Book Company, 1996)[74], page 3 he made the claim that he studied at *Umm ul-Qura'* in Makkah and *The Islāmic University of Madeenah* when this is false. Indeed, he miraculously now claims that he studied at "Madarasah Saltiyyah" and makes no mention of *Umm ul-Qura'* and *Madeenah University*!!? Clear *tadless* and *kadhib* (deception and lying)! See page 7 of one of his ebooks here: http://www.omarBakrī.info/Books/Ahlus%20Sunnah%20Wal%20Jamma.pdf – the link however no longer works!

- ✓ Still has not clearly repudiated his previous heretical beliefs of rejecting *ahad hadeeth* into *'aqeedah*.

- ✓ Still does not teach the books of the *'aqeedah* of the *Salaf* and is ignorant of them and omits aspects, such as the censure of revolting against the leaders and making *takfeer* of the Muslim rulers. Bakrī conveniently overlooks of the statements of the

Imāms in this issue. So for example on pp.51-64 he gives 15 attributes of *Ahl us-Sunnah* and yet fails to mention the issue of refraining from *takfeer* and *khurooj*!!

✓ Claims that Imām Ahmad ibn Hanbal *(rahimahullāh)* incited the common people against the rulers. In ftn.123 on page 111 of his ebook (on Ahl us-Sunnah which has been linked to above) Bakrī claims **"Imām Ahmed rose against and publically championed people against the state..."**!!?

✓ Still has not made any clarification of his heresies in Arabic, he has no books or works in Arabic and has rather deceived ignorant youth in the UK into blindly following him. The fact that even his website which is dedicated to him provides no link to any Arabic-twin site and his wasting time in conducting paltalk lectures in English to his blind followers in the UK indicates the true agenda of this man who now claims to be from the people of *Sunnah* in *'aqeedah* and *manhaj*. So where are his books in Arabic we ask? And where is the clarification of his errors in Arabic? Where is the explanation for his claims of studying at *Umm ul-Qura'* in Makkah and *The Islāmic University of Madeenah*? When the reality is that he was an employee for the company *Eastern Electric* owned by Shamsān and 'Abdul'Azeez as-Suhaybī in Riyadh. Then he went to the branch in Jeddah and during that time he did not study in any university, rather he went to America for a few months to study English and suddenly left and went to London and became the *Mufti* of *Hizb ut-Tahreer*.[75]

«2»

THE DIFFERENCES BETWEEN THE SALAFIS AND OMAR BAKRĪ'S CULT GROUPS (FROM "AL-MUHAJIROUN" TO THE "SALAFI YOUTH FOR ISLĀMIC PROPAGATION")

TOPIC (below)	Omar Bakrī, Anjem Choudhary and their Followers [some issues are also shared with other neo-Khawārij cults and new-age Takfeeris]	Salafis
Tawheed	*Tawheed* is referred to due to its status in Islām, yet its meaning is confined to the innovated matter of *al-Hākimyyah.* Slight referral to the statements of Imām Muhammad bin 'AbdulWahhāb in regards to *tawheed*, but not in detail. Emphasis on *al-Hākimiyyah* as a separate category, in keeping with the	*Hākimiyyah* is not a separate category rather it is a part of one of the following three categories of *tawheed* which are emphasised the *Salafis: Rubūbiyyah, Ulūhiyyah* and *Asmā wa's-Sifāt.* Along with the books of Imām Muhammad bin 'AbdulWahhab.[76] See explanations of these works by those contemporary Imāms who are the top experts in the

64

	Harakī-Takfīrī fascination of this issue as inherited from Sayyid Qutb. *Tawheed* is understood without the need of having to refer to those specialised in the field, rather Omar Bakrī Muhammad Fustuq is the only reference point in these matters and not those who have more knowledge of the works of Imām Muhammad bin 'AbdulWahhāb.	works of Imām Muhammad bin 'AbdulWahhāb, such as: Imām 'Abdul'Azeez bin Bāz, Imām Muhammad bin Sālih al-'Uthaymeen, Shaykh Sālih al-Fawzān, Shaykh Sālih Āli Shaykh and others. Shaykh 'Uthaymeen said about this *'Hākimiyyah'* concept: **"This statement is a newly-invented, innovated, evil saying, making the one who uses it repugnant...and it is indeed a misguided innovation."**[77]
Dealing with the Rulers [a]	Blanket *takfeer* is to be made of the rulers, without looking into the matters of *istihlāl*, *ibāha* or what actually constitutes *kufr*. Omar Bakrī in a book which is available	*Takfeer* has preventative factors which have to be safeguarded before a ruling can be made. *Takfeer* firstly is an exclusive matter which is performed only by the scholars and not any

Online entitled *The Islāmic Verdict on Jihad and the Method to Establish the Khlilafah,* and written during the al-Muhajiroun phase, states in his definition of **"Dār ul-Kufr"** that this also includes **"Muslim countries where Muslims have authority"** and cites Pakistan, Malaysia and Saudi Arabia as examples! Refer to: page 13 of the following:

http://osolihin.files.wordpress.com/2007/03/jihad-and-methodology.pdf

In the above document pp.11-15 Bakrī also makes up his own categories of the abodes with no source referencing layman, let alone by ignoramuses. In the Two Saheehs from Ibn 'Umar (radi Allāhu 'anhu) who said: the Messenger of Allāh (sallallāhu 'alayhi wassallam) said:

روي ان رسول الله صلى الله عليه وسلم قال: إذا قال الرجل لصاحبه "يا كافر" فإنها تجب على أحدهما. فإن كان الذي قيل له كافر فهو كافر. وإلا رجع إليه ما قال.

"Whenever a man says to his brother: "O kāfir!" then it applies to one of them or it returns to the one who actually said it first."[80]

	whatsoever! In a video on youtube Omar Bakrī praises a cult of death and makes *takfeer* of Saudi Arabia.[78] Anjem Choudhary stated in an interview with Press TV Channel on 20 March 2009: **"I think that the whole world today is governed by non-Islāmic law."**[79]	
Dealing with the Rulers [b]	The rulers are the cause of the problems in the Muslim world today. Recently, in a lecture entitled *'The Tawāgheet of Saudi Arabia'* found on the Islam4uk website, the speaker, an unknown and uncouth youth who goes by the fake name of 'Abū Turāb' for this lecture, says after 40 minutes	The rulers are a mere reflection of the people themselves.[81] It has been authenticated in *musnad* of Imām Ahmad and the *sunan* of Abū Dāwūd from Thawbān *(radi Allāhu 'anhu)* who said that the messenger of Allāh said: *"The nations will soon invite each other to attack you, just as people invite each other to eat from a dish."* Someone asked: *"Will that be because*

	and 50 seconds that: "Saudi Arabia is the leading country of shirk, kufr and bida'."	*of our small numbers at that time?"* He (sallallāhu 'alayhi wassallam) replied, *"No, you will be numerous at that time, but you will be like scum, like the scum and filth carried by a torrent, and Allāh will take fear from the hearts of your enemy and will place wahn into your hearts."* Someone asked, *"What is 'wahn' O messenger of Allāh?"* He (sallallāhu 'alayhi wassallam) replied, *"Love of the dunya and hatred for death."*
Dealings with the Kuffār [a]	No sort of dealings with *kuffār* are allowed whatsoever and are *kufr*.[82] But it is allowed to take welfare state benefits from them every two weeks as is in the process in the UK, along with utilising the	Dealings with the *kuffār* are allowed in certain circumstances with conditions which do not go against the Book of Allāh.[85] The Prophet Muhammad (sallallāhu 'alayhi wassallam) said: *"What is the condition of*

68

National Health Service and seeking council housing. In the 1996 documentary shown on Channel 4 entitled *Tottenham Ayatollah*, which Omar Bakrī freely and openly participated in, Bakrī on national TV (*Thursday Night Live*) openly admitted to being receipt of £150 per week in welfare state handouts, see 31 minutes into the documentary.[83]

Bakrī also says about the documentary-maker who is of Jewish background and his team that they are: **"his friends now and friends help each other out"**.[84]

This in itself would nullify the other extreme position

men who make conditions based on conditions which are not based on the Book of Allāh? Every condition which is not based on the Book of Allāh is invalid even if there are a hundred conditions. The book of Allāh is truer and the stipulation of Allāh is firmer." Refer to Sunan Ibn Mājah, vol.2, pp.842-843, no.2521.

	concerning *al-Walā wa'l-Barā'* but this is not to be questioned whatsoever. The bark is to be worse than the actual bite.	
Dealings with the Kuffār [b]	There can be no relationship whatsoever with the *kuffār*. However, since 2007 Omar Bakrī came to the realisation, based on what he took from the likes of Abū Baseer at-Tartūsī, that there is a "covenant" between Muslims and the non-Muslims.	Some relations with the *kuffār* are *kufr*, some are *harām* and some are *wājib*, some are permissible. For example, it is *kufr* to love a disbeliever on account of his *deen* and aid him in manifesting his *deen* over Muslims. It is allowed to love a disbeliever for a reason other than his *deen* and *'aqeedah*, such as when a Muslim man marries a chaste woman from the Jews or Christians, there is going to some natural love involved in such a relationship. So when Allāh allowed this, this

| | | indicates that this type of love of a non-Muslim is allowed. See Shaykh, Dr Muhammad bin 'Umar bin Sālim al-Bāzmūl (College of Da'wah and Usūl ud-Deen, Qur'ān and Sunnah Department, Umm ul-Qura University), *al-Walā' wa'l-Barā'* (Cairo: Dār ul-Istiqāmah, 1427 AH/2006 CE), p.13. It is also allowed to co-operate with *kuffār* in worldly affairs and in mutually exchanges such as buying, selling, trade, business, benefitting from their expertise, employing them and the likes. Rather this has a benefit for the Muslims and sevres the *deen*. We treat them well the *kuffār* who are good to us and there is also no problem in a Muslim man marrying a chaste Jewish |

		or Christian woman. Likewise, a Muslim child has to treat his non-Muslim parents well and give them their rights and within these examples (of marriage and parents) there is natural love involved. It is prohibited for a Muslim to resemble the *kuffār*. Refer to Shaykh, Dr Sālih bin Fawzān bin 'Abdullāh al-Fawzān, *Sharh Risālat ud-Dalā'il fee Hukm Muwalāt Ahl Ashrāk li'sh-Shaykh Sulaymān bin 'Abdullāh Muhammad 'AbdulWahhāb* (n.p., 1428 AH/2007 CE)
Dealings with the Kuffār [c]	All *kuffār* are against the *deen* and thus there can be no agreements and the like with them, unless Omar Bakrī Muhammad realises that there can be some dealings with them.	The *kuffār* are of different types and thus are to be treated accordingly. Ibn ul-Qayyim stated: **"The kuffār are either: Ahl ul-Harb, Ahl ul-'Ahd or Ahl ul-Amān. Three categories: Ahl udh-**

		Dhimmah, Ahl ul-Hudnah and Ahl ul-Amān." Refer to Ibn ul-Qayyim, *Ahkām Ahl udh-Dhimmah*, vol.2, p.873.
Istiʿānah biʾl-Kuffār (Seeking assistance from non-Muslims)	Not allowed at any time whatsoever and is *kufr*. Inherited from the post-*Hizb ut-Tahreer* and early *'al-Muhajiroun'* phase. Indeed, it is the "worst sin" as stated by some former and current followers of Omar Bakrī up to this day. Recently in London, an *al-Muhajrioun* defector, former Omar Bakrī Muhammad cult member and now philosophy student at *Birkbeck University*,[86] stated in a dialogue with some Salafis in London that allowing	Is allowed at certain times with conditions, as the Messenger of Allāh *(sallallāhu 'alayhi wassallam)* enlisted the help of 'Abdullāh bin 'Uraqit al-Laythī, while he was a disbeliever. So help from them is also allowed at times.[87]

	the US troops into Saudi Arabia was "the biggest sin"?!! There is no doubt therefore that even after his defection from Bakrī's *al-Muhajiroun* the individual has still retained some of Omar Bakrī Muhammad's teachings.	
Jihad	**Anyone who fights the Kuffār is regarded instantly as a "Mujāhid"** and is supported regardless of who they are as long as they claim they are waging jihad. Jihad is generally not to be actually waged but support is to be given to whomsoever claims to be doing it around the world.[88]	Jihad has core principles and types. The Divinely Legislated Jihad is legislated due to other corroborating factors, which is establishing the *deen* of Allāh in the earth. Before calling to it (Jihad) there must be the presence of the Divinely Legislated detailed *fiqh* along with deep and lengthy analysis. From the particular affairs in comprehending the

condition of the Muslims is that if they are weak due to their numbers, or due to their lack of preparation in relation to their enemies, it is not correct for them to tread the path of armed jihad against the enemy due to their condition of weakness. What makes this apparent is the fact that Allāh did not instruct His Messenger (sallallāhu alayhi wassallam) and the Companions (radi Allāhu 'anhum) to fight the kuffār when they were in Makkah due to their weakness in number and in readiness in relation to their enemies.[89]

Ibn Taymiyyah said:

"It was instructed to abstain from fighting them due to his inability and the inability of the

Muslims. Then when they migrated to Madeenah and gained assistance, Allāh permitted him to make (armed) jihad and then when they grew in strength Allāh prescribed fighting for them. Yet Allāh did not prescribe fighting beforehand for their own safety as they were not able to fight all of the kuffār. But when Allāh opened up Makkah for them and halted fighting against the Quraysh and the kings of the Arabs and a delegation of Arabs came into Islām, Allāh instructed the Prophet (sallallāhu alayhi wassallam) with fighting all of the kuffār except those who had a temporal bond of agreement and Allāh instructed him to annul those absolute

		agreements and that which annulled it was leaving fighting." Refer to: Ibn Taymiyyah, *al-Jawāb as-Saheeh*, vol.1, p.237.
Terrorists	Terrorists are good and they should be supported and protected according to Omar Bakrī.[90] The attackers on 9/11 are the **"magnificent 19"** and should be referred to as such, as stated on national British TV for example by Abū 'Uzayr of Leyton, East London.	Terrorists are motivated by emotions and haste which as a result leads them to extreme acts of violence wherein Muslims and non-Muslims are killed in the process of them trying to achieve their aims. They are misguided and ignorant of jihad and its principles. Allāh says **"Fight in the way of Allāh those who fight you but do not transgress. Indeed. Allāh does not like transgressors."** *{Baqara (2): 190}*

| Targeting Innocent People in Warfare | Indiscriminate suicide bombings, which target innocent people, are not to be condemned as there are proofs for this, refer to words of Anjem Choudhary here: http://news.bbc.co.uk/1/hi/programmes/hardtalk/3014703.stm Non-Muslim children are not innocent according to Omar Bakrī.[91] "Martyrdom operations" are **"completely praiseworthy"** as Abū Izzaddeen stated in his interview on *Newsnight* with Richard Watson in September 2006.[92] Asif Mohammed Hanif, along with Omar Khan Sharif, who blew himself up at a Cafe in Tel Aviv, was a member of "al-Muhajiroun." | Non-Muslim civilians are not to be targeted in warfare. From Buraydah *(radi Allāhu 'anhu)* that the Messenger of Allāh *(sallallāhu 'alayhi wassallam)* used to say[93]: *"Fight in the way of Allāh and fight those who disbelieve in Allāh. Do battle and do not exceed the limits, do not depart (from the battle), do not mutilate and do not kill children or those in monasteries (i.e. places of worship)."*[94] Abū Bakr as-Siddeeq *(radi Allāhu 'anhu)* said to Yazeed bin Abī Sufyān *(radi Allāhu 'anhu)* when he sent him to Shām, *"You will surely find a people who claim to have secluded themselves for Allāh, so leave them to what they claim they have secluded themselves for and I advise you with ten* |

Those guilty of the "Crevice plot" to use fertiliser bombs to blow up the Bluewater Shopping Centre and Ministry of Sound nightclub in central London were linked to the cult of Omar Bakrī Muhammad.

Muhammad Junaid Babar of Queens (New York), was a cult follower of Omar Bakrī Muhammad and then turned Supergrass and informant for the FBI and gave the full details of the links, being a "star witness" for the prosecution.

Muhammad Junaid Babar was given immunity from prosecution in regards to the charges against the British al-

matters: do not kill women, children, the elderly and infirm. Do not chop down the fruit-bearing trees. Do not destroy inhabited places. Do not slaughter sheep or camels except for food. Do not burn bees and do not scatter them. Do not steal from the booty and do not be cowardly."[95]

See: Shaykh Hamad bin Ibrāheem al-'Uthmān, *Jihād: Anwā'ahu wa Ahkāmuhu, wa'l-Hadd al-Fāsil Baynahu wa Bayna'l-Fawda* ('Ammān: Dār ul-Athariyyah, 1428 AH/2007 CE), pp.220-28.

The story of the people of Tā'if being attacked with *manjaneeq* is not relayed with an authentic *sanad*.[96]

	Muhajiroun cult followers involved. Due to these events however, the line is that innocents within the UK are not to be attack as there is a "covenant" between the country and Muslims.	
Non-Muslim Governments	Enmity is to be shown towards this country without having to make *hijrah* from it and without necessarily having to target UK citizens on their shores. One can still sit here claiming the *DHSS* from non-Muslim governments and receiving financial support from them. Condemnation and political agitation does not impede the	The Western non-Muslim government are disbelievers and as a result do things which are against the *deen*. If a Muslim freely chooses to live under a non-Muslim government he should maintain good relations with his neighbours and give them *da'wah*. Furthermore, the Muslim has an agreement of safety and trust ('Ahd ul-Amān) with such non-Muslims which he cannot

	"covenant" between the UK and cult followers.	renege upon. If a Muslim does not like living under the non-Muslim government then he should leave it immediately, get out and go to live in a Muslim country. A Muslim should not sit there taking welfare state benefit handouts every two weeks and council houses from the non-Muslim government and at the same time complain about it. Speaking about any government is *harām* if it will bring about harm. No benefit is gained by merely saying any ridiculous thing just for the sake of "speaking out". Refer to audio lectures by Shaykh, Dr Khālid al-Anbaree on *Politics in Light of Islām* at www.salafimanhaj.com

Politics	Extremism in dealing with the foreign policies of the British government and manipulation of this in order to whip the Muslims up into a frenzy, as inherited from *Hizb ut-Tahreer*. The *deen* is used excessively in order to put forward political aims.	Those in authority over the Muslims are in charge of the political arena primarily. Political discussion is not given precedence over *tawheed* and it is never used to rally the Muslims.[97] As for extremism in this regard then the Messenger of Allāh *(sallallāhu 'alayhi wassallam)* said on the authority of Ibn 'Abbās *(radi Allāhu 'anhu)*: *"Beware of extremism in the religion! For the people before you were destroyed due to extremism in the religion."* Recorded by Ibn Mājah,[98] an-Nasā'ī,[99] Ibn Khuzaymah authenticated the hadeeth[100] as did Ibn Hibbān[101] and al-Hākim and adh-Dhahabī agreed.[102]

Demonstrations, Protests and Rallies: "The Public Da'wah" [a]	Allowed and part of commanding the good in London and the wider UK, regardless of the consequences and the negative image they give over, as inherited from *Hizb ut-Tahreer*. Also regardless of the fact that no credible scholar of the Sunnah has deduced that demonstrations, protests and rallies are a Divinely Legislated means for rectification. 'Umar and Hamza *(radi Allāhu 'anhum)* "marched" as reported in some narrations and this is proof that marches, rallies, protests and demonstrations are allowed. Moreover, protests and rallies are good	Allāh says,

﴿ادْعُ إِلَى سَبِيلِ رَبِّكَ بِالْحِكْمَةِ وَالْمَوْعِظَةِ الْحَسَنَةِ وَجَـٰدِلْهُم بِالَّتِي هِيَ أَحْسَنُ إِنَّ رَبَّكَ هُوَ أَعْلَمُ بِمَن ضَلَّ عَن سَبِيلِهِ وَهُوَ أَعْلَمُ بِالْمُهْتَدِينَ﴾

"Invite to the way of your Lord with wisdom and good instruction, and argue with them in a way that is best. Indeed, your Lord is most knowing of who has strayed from His way, and He is most knowing of who is [rightly] guided."

{an-Nahl (16): 125}

Allāh also instructed Mūsā in regards to the Pharaoh, the leader of *kufr*, *shirk*, *dhulm* and *tughyān* of his day:

﴿فَقُولَا لَهُ قَوْلاً لَّيِّناً لَّعَلَّهُ يَتَذَكَّرُ أَوْ يَخْشَى﴾

"And speak to him with |

	publicity stunts for the cult. Demonstrations can involve any slogan that attracts attention and rabble-rouses. Therefore, banners and slogans which state the following are allowed: **"behead those who insult Islām", "be prepared for the real holocaust", "slay those who insult Islām"** and **"O Muslims be with the terrorists", "Europe Europe you will pay, the fantastic four are on their way"**. See: http://news.bbc.co.uk/ 1/hi/programmes/new snight/4700976.stm Dressing up as suicide bombers and flag-burning, in order to enrage the *kuffār*, are also totally legitimate	**gentle speech that perhaps he may be reminded or fear [Allāh].""** *{TāHā (20): 44}* Demonstrations are an innovation which have no basis and are not from the methodology of the *Salaf* in calling to Allāh, hence none of the 'Ulama of Ahl us-Sunnah sanction them. The Companions *(radi Allāhu 'anhum)* did not march or protest in the streets screaming words of political incitement directed at those in authority, their enemies and others who were antagonistic to the *deen*. The narrations which state that 'Umar and Hamza "marched" are *da'eef* (weak) due to the presence of Ishāq bin Abī

84

and part of the **"public da'wah"**. As done by Omar Khayam of Bedford, a convicted crack cocaine dealer who was out on parole and attended a Bakrī-inspired demonstration in London in 2006 dressed in this way. Slogans such as **"Khaybar, Khaybar yā Yahood"** were utilized at a demonstration by Omar Bakrī's cult followers in New York from the so-called *'Islāmic Thinkers Society'* in May 2008.[103]

Farwah in the *isnad* and he is Matrook. See Ibn Hajr, *at-Taqreeb*, p.102 and *al-Isābah*, vol.4, p.280.

Demonstrations are based on the futile methodologies of non-believing socialists and anarchists. Since when has a demonstration benefitted any political party or group? The Salafi Imām 'Abdul'Azeez bin Bāz *(rahimahullāh)* stated:

"A good method is of the greatest means for acceptance of the truth. While a bad and violent method is of the most dangerous means for rejection of the truth and for a lack of accepting it, it can cause unrest, oppression, enmity and tension.

The demonstrations that some people do are

		connected to this as they cause serious evils for the preachers (du'āt), as do protests in the streets. Demonstrations are not the way to rectify situations and give da'wah.
		Rather the correct way is to visit and write in a way that is better and advise the leader, ruler or tribal Shaykh without violence and demonstrating.
		The Prophet (sallallāhu 'alayhi wassallam) remained in Makkah for thirteen years and neither demonstrated or protested nor threatened to destroy people's properties or assassinate people."[104]
		Shaykh Sālih al-Fawzān stated in regards to a question that was posed to him about staging

| | | | protests and demonstrations and if they are to be considered Jihād:

There is no benefit in demonstrations – it is just commotion. They are a type of disorder. How will it cause harm to the enemy if the people go out and demonstrate in one of the streets raising their voices? Rather, this is from the things that will only make the enemy pleased and happy. Thus he (the enemy) will say: "This has harmed and hurt them." So the enemy will rejoice. Islām is a religion of tranquility and calmness; it is a religion of knowledge. It is not a religion of clamor and commotion. It is a religion that strives to achieve tranquility and calmness, |

while at the same time, (encourages) doing deeds that are of benefit and praise, such as providing support for the Muslims, supplicating for them and providing them with money and weapons. This is praiseworthy. And also (what is beneficial is) arguing on their behalf to the various countries that the oppression they are in be uplifted and requesting from these countries, which claim to have democracy, that these Muslims be given their due rights. And humanitarian rights are what these people boast so much about. However, according to them the only human is the disbeliever, whereas the Muslim in their eyes is not a human being – he is a terrorist! They call the Muslims terrorists! And the human being that has (humanitarian) rights, according to them, is the disbeliever!

So the Muslims must follow and adhere to the methodology Islām has prescribed with regard to these occurrences and other situations. Islām did not come with demonstrations, shouting and raising voices. It did not prescribe destroying property or committing violations. Yes, all of this is neither part of Islām nor does this bring about any benefit. This only causes harm to the Muslims and it does not harm the enemy. This only harms the Muslims and it does not harm their enemy. In fact, their

		enemy rejoices at this and says (to himself): "I have affected them", "I have made them angry" and "I have influenced them."[105]
Khilāfah	The Prophetic Khilāfah ended on March 3rd 1924 CE. This has been mentioned by cult followers such as "Abū Farruq" of Luton, in a recent lecture entitled 'The Devil's Deception of the Reformist'.[106] Apparently, a day before this dismantling there was a Prophetic Khilāfah, the belief as inherited from Hizb ut-Tahreer. It was also stated by another ignorant cult follower.[107]	Ahmad bin Munee'ah narrated from Suraij bin Nu'mān who narrated from Hashraj bin Nubātah on the authority of Sa'eed bin Jamhān who said: Safeenah said: the Messenger of Allāh (sallallāhu 'alayhi wassalam) said, "The Khilāfah in my Ummah will be thirty (30) years, and then after it there will be kingship." Refer to Saheeh Sunan at-Tirmidhī, vol.2, p.486 no.2226 and Imām al-Albānī said the hadeeth is Saheeh.[108] As for the Ottoman "Caliphate" then it was an empire which by Omar Bakrī's own takfīrī standards would have

		easily qualified as an apostate state due to its seeking help and assistance from disbelieving states during the Crimean war, not to mention its involvement in grave-worship! Refer to Shaykh, Dr Sālih bin Fawzān bin 'Abdullāh al-Fawzān, *Sharh Risālat ud-Dalā'il fee Hukm Muwalāt Ahl Ashrāk li'sh-Shaykh Sulaymān bin 'Abdullāh Muhammad 'AbdulWahhāb* (n.p., 1428 AH/2007 CE), pp.15, 41-46, 49.
Commanding the Good and Forbidding the Evil: "Public Da'wah" [b]	As inherited from *Hizb ut-Tahreer*, the good has to be enjoined even if it may bring about potential harm. It is to be used as a slogan without fully implementing it correctly as the classical scholars have	Abū Sa'eed Al-Khudrī *(radi Allāhu 'anhu)* said: I heard the Messenger of Allāh *(sallallāhu 'alayhi wassallam)* say: *"Whosoever of you sees an evil action, let him change it with his hand; and if he is unable to do so, then with his tongue; and if he is unable to*

highlighted in their books. Ranting, raving and rabble-rousing are all legitimate forms of enjoining the good and forbidding evil, regardless of whether such activities bring about any harm upon the entire Muslim community. There are no principles for commanding the good and forbidding the evil, the "good" is to be commanded no matter what. To not command the good due to harm is an excuse to leave an obligation. Refer to lecture entitled *Benefit and Harm* by "Abū Ibrahim" an Omar Bakrī follower.[109] The false, revolutionary principle of:	*do so, then with his heart; and that is the weakest of īmān."* Recorded in Saheeh Muslim. Forbidding the evil is always given precedence over its sister half of enjoining the good, unless the good, outweighs the evil. Furthermore, there is *fiqh* to this issue.[110] Attention has to be paid to the *fiqh* principle of: *dafa' al-mafāsid muqaddim 'ala ijtilāb il-masālih* also referred to as *dar' al-mafāsid awlā min jalb ul-masālih* (averting harms take precedence over obtaining benefits). Along with taking into consideration the *fiqh* of *Ma'alat* (end results and consequences). Also from the conditions of commanding the good and forbidding the evil

| | الغاية تبرر الوسيلة "the ends justify the means", inherited from other *Harakī-Takfīrīs* applies. | are: capability and security. Refer to Ibn Taymiyyah, *Majmū' al-Fatāwā*, vol.28, p.66. |

Al-Hāfidh Abū Bakr al-Khallāl (d. 311 AH/923 CE) reported that Imām Ahmed was asked about commanding good and forbidding evil when one is in a state of fear:

أخبرنا حرب بن إسماعيل قال سمعت إسحاق بن راهويه حدثهم أن أبا عبدالله سئل: الأمر بالمعروف والنهي عن المنكر واجب على المسلم؟ قال: نعم قال: فإن خشي؟ قال هو واجب عليه حتى يخاف فإذا خشي على نفسه فلا يفعل

"Harb bin Isma'īl informed us: he said I heard Ishāq bin Rahawayh narrating to them that Abū 'Abdillāh was asked: [is] commanding the good and forbidding the evil

| | | obligatory on the Muslim? He said yes. He said and if he fears?
He said it is obligatory for him until he fears. If he fears for himself, he does not do it."
Refer to al-Hāfidh Abū Bakr Ahmad bin Muhammad bin Hāroon al-Khallāl (d. 234-311 AH/CE), eds. Mashhūr bin Hasan bin Mahmood Āl Salmān and Hishām bin Ismā'īl as-Saqā, *Kitāb al-'Amr bi'l-Ma'roof wa'n-Nahy 'an al-Munkar* ('Amman and Beirut: Dār ul-'Ammār and al-Maktab al-Islāmi, 1410 AH/1990 CE), p.25.[111]
Ibn ul-Qayyim said:
"[Based on its effects] forbidding the evil has four levels:
The first level is that the evil would end and be replaced by its opposite |
| --- | --- | --- |

		[i.e. good]. The second level is that it [the evil] will diminish without ending completely. The third is that the evil will be replaced by [an evil] equivalent to it and this is liable to ijtihād. The fourth level is that the evil will be replaced by an evil worse than it. The first two levels conform with the Shariah; the third is liable to ijtihad (scholarly judgement) and the fourth is prohibited." See Ibn ul-Qayyim, *I'lam al-Muwaqqi'een*, pp.22-24
Source References for Understanding the Deen [a]	The Qur'ān and Sunnah, in a restricted sense, based on the understanding of Omar Bakrī Muhammad Fustuq primarily and then based on snippets	The Qur'ān and Sunnah, in its totality, in accordance with the understanding of the *Salaf us-Sālih*. The Messenger of Allāh *(sallallāhu 'alayhi wassallam)* made clear that the best of people are his

	from the understanding of the neo-Khawārij.	generation and then those who come after them, he said *(sallallāhu alayhi wassallam)*: *"The best of people are my generation, then those who come after them and then those come after them."*[112]
Source References for Understanding the Deen [b]: Understanding the Creed (which includes issues of how to deal with the rulers)	Whatever Omar Bakrī Muhammad Fustuq composes, this will change in accordance with the desires of Omar Bakrī.	The early books of creed such as: *Usūl us-Sunnah* of Imām Ahmad bin Hanbal; *Sharh us-Sunnah* of Imām al-Muzanī (d. 264 AH); *as-Sunnah* by Imām Abdullāh bin Ahmad bin Hanbal (d. 290 AH); *Sareeh us-Sunnah* by Imām Ibn Jareer at-Tabaree (d. 310 AH); *Sharh us-Sunnah* by Imām al-Barbahārī (d. 329 AH); *ash-Sharee'ah* by Imām Abū Bakr al-Ājurrī (d. 360 AH); *I'tiqād Ahl us-Sunnah* by Imām Abū Bakr al-Ismā'īlī (d. 371 AH); *Sharh Usūl I'tiqād Ahl ns-Sunnah wal-Jamā'ah* by Imām al-

		Lālikā'ī (d.418H); *'Aqeedah us-Salaf wa As-hāb ul-Hadeeth* by Imām Abū Uthmān as-Sābūnī (449 AH).
Source References for Understanding the Deen [c]: Ijtihād	Omar Bakrī Muhammad Fustuq is a fully qualified scholar entirely capable of *ijtihād*, as inherited from *Hizb ut-Tahreer* misinformation.	*Ijtihād* has conditions, so it is *harām* for a man to make *ijtihād* until the conditions of *ijtihād* have been maintained.[113] Some of the conditions for *ijtihād* are: - Maturity and intelligence, as *ijtihād* is worship. - Strong understanding to be able to make *istinbāt* (deductions). - Strong memorisation of the intended issues along with memorisation of the *Shari'* texts, or at least strong

		understanding and familiarity with the source *Shari'* texts.
		- 'Ilm of what the sciences one is seeking to derive a ruling from is based upon. These sciences are knowledge of the Book of Allāh and of the *ayahs* related to the *ahkām*; knowledge of the *nāsikh* and *mansookh* from the Book of Allāh; knowledge of the general and specific; knowledge of *al-Itlāq* and *at-Taqyeed*; knowledge of *ahādeeth*, which explains the

| | | Qur'ān and what is *Saheeh* and *da'eef* from them, along with knowledge of the *ahad* narrations and the *mutawātir*; knowledge of *Usūl* and the *Qawā'id* of *fiqh*; knowledge of the Arabic language, grammar, morphology and *bayān*; knowledge of the *furū' fiqhiyyah*. |
| | | - The above are the conditions for a Mujtahid Madhhab who has to know what those of his madhhab have concurred and outlined in accordance with |

		the *Usūl* of the Imām of the madhhab. Refer to Imām Ibn 'Āsim al-Ghranātī al-Mālikī, ed. Fakhruddeen bin az-Zubayr bin 'Ali al-Mahasī, *Sharh Nudhum Murtaqā al-Wusūl ila 'Ilm il-Usūl* ('Ammān, Jordan: Dār ul-Athariyyah, 1428 AH/2007 CE), pp.772-774. also see az-Zarkashī, eds. Panel of Ulama from al-Azhar, *al-Bahr ul-Muheet* (Dār ul-Khānī, 1414 AH, 1st Edn.), vol.8, p.237 The more correct opinion with the scholars of *Usūl* is that *ijtihād* has parts, so a person can make *ijtihād* in some issues but not in others as *ijtihād* has types.[114]
Source References for Understanding	Omar Bakrī Muhammad Fustuq is to be followed and is the main source	The Qur'ān and Sunnah are the main references to refer back to. A Muslim, if

the Deen [d]: Taqleed	of reference to go back to for matters related to Islām. He is to be followed uncritically. However, publically it is to be asserted that taqleed is forbidden.[115]	able, should research the evidences. The Messenger of Allāh (sallallāhu 'alayhi wassallam) stated: "I have left two things among you which you will not be misguided after them, the Book of Allāh and my Sunnah." The hadeeth is reported by al-Hākim and is Saheeh. Shaykh ul-Islām Ibn Taymiyyah said: "It has been verified in the Book, Sunnah and Ijmā' that Allāh has obligated the creation to obey Him and His Messenger and He did not obligate this Ummah to obey anyone else specifically in all that he instructs and forbids, except for the Messenger of Allāh (sallallāhu 'alayhi wassallam). They also agreed that no one is infallible in all that he commands and forbids

		except for the Messenger of Allāh (sallallāhu 'alayhi wassallam). For this reason, more than one of the Imāms has said: 'every person has their statement accepted or rejected except for the Messenger of Allāh.'" See Shaykh ul-Islām Ibn Taymiyyah, *Majmū' al-Fatāwā*, vol.20, p.210. Ibn Taymiyyah also said: "As for the obligation of following a speaker in every single thing that he says without mentioning the evidence for the accuracy of what he says, then this is not correct. Rather this level is only for the Messenger of Allāh which is only suitable for him (sallallāhu 'alayhi wassallam)." See Shaykh ul-Islām Ibn Taymiyyah, *Majmū' al-Fatāwā*, vol.35,

		p.121.
Manhaj	This changes as often as a baby changes its nappies, based on the political zeitgeist and also depending on whatever Omar Bakrī Muhammad Fustuq cooks up whenever it tickles his fancy and desires.	Does not change with the times, rather is based on the Qur'ān, Sunnah and *Salaf us-Sālih*. The Prophet *(sallallāhu 'alayhi wassallam)* instructed his followers to follow his Sunnah and the Sunnah of the Khulafā' ar-Rāshideen and he *(sallallāhu 'alayhi wassallam)* warned against opposing them, he said: *"Stick to my Sunnah and the Sunnah of the Rightly guided Caliphs after me. Hold firm to it and bite onto it with the molars, and beware of newly invented matters for every newly-invented matter is an innovation and every innovation is misguidance."*[116] Imām Ahmad *(rahimahullāh)* said:

		"The Foundations of the Sunnah with us are: Holding firm to what the Companions of the Messenger of Allāh (sallallāhu alayhi wassallam) and following them and abandoning innovation."[117] Ibn ul-Qayyim said: Whoever spreads statements or forms principles based on his understanding and interpretation then it is not obligatory for the Ummah to follow this or to refer judgement to this (i.e. the man's own principles and interpretations) until it is compared to what the Messenger of Allāh (sallallāhu 'alayhi wassallam) came with. If it agrees with it and its authenticity, and is

		authenticated, then at that time it (i.e. a person's own principles and interpretations) will be accepted, but if it opposes what the Messenger of Allāh came with then it will be rejected and discarded. If none of these sides are clarified then the matter becomes deferred (and one should hesitate in making a definite decision). The best case is that it is allowed to accept such views and issue fatāwā based on them, or they can be rejected.[118]
The 'Ulama [a]	The Muslim scholars are all **"scholars for dollars"** and **"government scholars"**, and as a result are not to be trusted. Therefore, only Omar	The 'Ulama are to be respected and their guidance is important,[119] Narrated 'Abdullāh Ibn 'Amr Ibn al-'Ās *(radi Allāhu 'anhu):* "I heard Allāh's Messenger *(sallallāhu*

	Bakrī Muhammad Fustuq is a trustworthy source along with other assorted speakers who agree with him.	*alayhi wasallam)* saying: *"Allāh does not take away the knowledge by taking it away from (the hearts of) the people, but He takes it away by the death of the scholars till when none (of the scholars) remains. People will then take as their leaders ignorant people who when consulted will give their verdicts without knowledge. So, they will go astray and will lead others astray."*[120] Aboo Hurayrah *(radi Allāhu 'anhu)* narrated that the Messenger of Allāh *(sallallāhu alayhi wassallam)* said: *"There will come upon the people years of deceit wherein the liar will be regarded as truthful and the truthful will be considered a liar and the dishonest will be trusted and the trustworthy one will be considered dishonest and the*

		Ruwaybidah will begin to speak!" Then it was asked: *"What are the Ruwaybidah?"* He *(sallallāhu alayhi wassallam)* replied: *"The foolish insignificant man who speaks about general affairs."*[121]
The 'Ulama [b]	The only scholars to be referred to are Omar Bakrī Muhammad Fustuq, who is the primary source to be followed as he is a *Mufti* and *Mujtahid*, in keeping with what was inherited from *Hizb ut-Tahreer UK* in the mid-1990s. Other options for knowledge are 'Abdullāh Faisal al-Jamaykī,[122] Anwar al-Awlaki,[123] Abū Qatādah[124] and Abū Baseer at-Tartūsī.[125]	The Prophet *(sallallāhu 'alayhi wassallam)* feared for his Ummah the Imāms of misguidance, he said *(sallallāhu 'alayhi wassallam): "What I fear for my Ummah are the Imāms of misguidance."*[126] He warned about them in the context of the *hadeeth* about the Dajjāl when he *(sallallāhu 'alayhi wassallam)* said: *"I fear for you other matters besides the Dajjāl."*[127] The contemporary Salafi scholars of the Sunnah of the recent period are: Imām Muhammad

		Nāsiruddeen al-Albānī; Imām 'Abdul'Azeez bin Bāz; Imām Muhammad bin Sālih al-'Uthaymeen, Imām Muqbil ibn Hādī al-Wādi'ī, al-'Allāmah Sālih al-Fawzān, al-Ma'ālī Sālih Āli Shaykh, Shaykh al-Mufti 'Abdul'Azeez Āli Shaykh, Shaykh al-Qādī Sālih al-Luhaydān, Shaykh 'AbdulMuhsin al-'Abbād al-Badr, Shaykh Rabī' bin Hādī al-Madkhalī, Shaykh Wasiullāh al-'Abbās, Shaykh al-Imām 'Abdullāh bin 'Abdul'Azeez al-'Aqeel, Shaykh Ihsān Ilahi Thaheer, Shaykh Badīuddeen Shāh as-Sindī and many more which would be too many to list here.
Khabr ul-Āhād	It was denied initially by Omar Bakrī	The acceptance of Khabr ul-Ahad has been constant

108

Muhammad, despite the heretical basis of such a denial. It included not taking *ahād* narrations into *'aqeedah* which would mean denying punishment in the grave and many other areas of creed. Acceptance of *ahād* narrations were then later included as a core aspect of *'aqeedah*, in keeping with Ahl us-Sunnah. The shakiness in this regard is not to be questioned.

amongst the people of the Sunnah since the time of the Messenger, which itself is a conclusive evidence, since the people of the Sunnah will never unite upon a falsehood. The Messenger of Allāh (*sallallāhu 'alayhi wassallam*) sent Mua'dh (*radi Allāhu 'anhu*) as a single conveyor to the people of the book with matters pertaining to creed.[128]

Khabr ul-Āhād is a proof in matters of *'aqeedah* and *ahkām* and there is no distinction. Ibn 'AbdulBarr stated:

"Within the entire creed regarding Allāh's Names and Attributes there is nothing except that which has been documented in the Book of Allāh, authenticated from the

		Messenger of Allāh, agreed upon by the Ummah and has been transmitted from Akhbār ul-Āhād. All of this has to be submitted to and accepted and not to be looked into (i.e. questioned)." See Ibn 'AbdulBarr, *Jāmi' Bayān ul-'Ilm wa Fadlihi*, vol.2, p.96.
Forming Partisan Political Groups and Parties	Omar Bakrī Muhammad sanctions this and it involves changing name as often as necessary in order to resurface under a different name yet still preach the same message of political agitation, *takfeer*, mayhem and chaos. All the while, total allegiance is to be given to Omar Bakrī	One of the main causes of division and tribulation has been the existence of parties and groups which have partisan loyalties to innovators and desires which oppose the Sunnah and have biased and bigoted partisanship to personalities and groups. *Salafis* do not hold secret clandestine meetings in order to put into place a strategic political plan.

110

	Muhammad and then Anjem Choudhary.	Pledging allegiance to heads of organisations, groups and political parties is partisanship. Shaykh ul-Islām Ibn Taymiyyah stated: **"As for the "head of the hizb" then he is the lead of the group which forms partisanship, meaning: the group which becomes a party. If they are gathered upon what Allāh and His Messenger have instructed, without adding or subtracting anything, then they are believers and unto them is what is unto them and upon them what is upon them. Yet if they add or subtract, like for example by having biased bigotry in truth and falsehood, to whoever joins their hizb and turning away from whoever does not join**

		their hizb, whether in truth or falsehood – then this is division that Allāh and His Messenger have censured." See: Shaykh ul-Islām Ibn Taymiyyah, *Majmū' al-Fatāwā*, vol.11, p.92. Also refer to: a. Sheikh Ali ibn Hasan Ali ibn Abdul Hameed, trans. Aboo Talhah Dawud Burbank, *Muslim Unity in the Light of Numerous Groups and Parties* (Birmingham: Salafi Publications). b. Shaykh 'AbdulMālik ar-Ramadānī, *Madarik un-Nadhr fi's-Siyasah: Bayna't-Tatbiqat ash-Shar'iyyah wa'l-Infia'lat al-Hamasiyyah* [Perceptions of Viewing Politics: Between the Divinely Legislated Application and Enthusiastic

		Disturbances], (KSA: Dar Sabeel il-Mumineen, 1418 AH/1997 CE, 2nd Edn).
Tāghūt	*Tawāgheet* are the rulers, as emphasised by Omar Bakrī Muhammad Fustuq. In the vastness of the issue of *tāghoot* and its types, attention is only given to discussing one type of *tāghūt*, that being the tyrannical *hākim* (ruler). Fundamental issues are left, in order to emphasise a political definition. They indiscriminately charge every single Muslim ruler with being a *tāghoot* without taking into consideration *istihlāl, ibāha* and the impediments of *takfeer*. This conclusively	All definitions are embraced and they remain faithful to all classical definitions of *tawāghīt* without restricting them or utilising them for political means. As Salafis do not hold that by removing the rulers by force this will alleviate the predicament in which Muslims have found themselves. Al-Qurtubī *(rahimahullah)* stated in his *tafseer* of *ayah* 36 of Surat un-Nahl **"And We certainly sent into every nation a messenger, [saying], "Worship Allāh and avoid tāghūt.""**: **"Means: leave all that is worshipped other than Allāh like Shaytān, the**

	proves that they are all about politics, revolution and rulers, as just as they have done with *tawheed* by restricting it they have done with the definition of *tāghūt*.[129]	fortune-teller, the idol and all who call to misguidance." Al-Fayrūzabādī *(rahimahullāh)* stated in *al-Qāmūs* under the item *'taghā'*: "And at-Tāghūt: al-Lāt, al-'Uzza, the fortune-teller, Shaytān, and every leader of misguidance, the idols and whatever is worshipped by other than Allāh, this is attributed to Ahl ul-Kitāb." Ar-Rāghib al-Asfahānī *(rahimahullāh)* stated in *Mufradāt Alfādh ul-Qur'ān*,[130] p.108 under the item *'tāghā'*: "At-Tāghūt is an expression for: every transgressor and all that is worshipped other than Allāh...and based on what has preceded: the magician, fortune-teller,

		the defiant jinn and the one who averts from the way of goodness – are all named as "tāghūt"."
		Imām Muhammad bin 'AbdulWahhāb *(rahimahullāh)* stated in *ad-Durur*, vol.1, p.137:
		"The Tawāgheet are many and what is clear to us are five: the first is Shaytān, then the tyrannical leader, the one who takes a bribe, the one who is worshipped and is pleased with that and the one who acts without knowledge."
		Imām Ibn 'Uthaymeen *(rahimahullāh)* stated in *Sharh ul-Usūl uth-Thalātha* (Riyadh: Dār uth-Tharayā, 1420 AH/2000 CE), p.151:
		"and the 'Ulama of evil are those who call to misguidance and kufr or call to bida' (innovation) or call to making halal

		what Allāh has made harām, or make harām what Allāh has made halāl - all are tawāghīt." Therefore, a caller and leader of misguidance and innovation can also be rendered as a *tāghūt*!

«3»
IS ANJEM CHOUDHARY A QUALIFIED ISLĀMIC JUDGE OF A SHARIAH COURT IN THE UK? FROM YUPPIE TO QĀDĪ IN A YEAR![131]

The following was advertised in early 2008:

Britain under Islām Conference, Saturday 9th February 2008, 6pm - 7:30pm, Venue: Harmony Hall, Truro Road, Walthamstow, E17 7BY, **Speaker: Anjem Choudary, Judge of the Shari'ah Court of the UK and Principal Lecturer at the London School of Shari'ah.**

Not only is this is a very bold claim to promote among the Muslims but as one can immediately observe from Choudhary's media antics, his Islāmic knowledge is negligible to say the least! At this point then, before we assess the credentials of Anjem Choudhary, it is worth us taking a look at what the scholars of the past have outlined as the criterion for a *Qādī*, a position which Anjem Choudhary now claims to hold!? Indeed, while it is known that he was a fully qualified solicitor of secular British law this in no way gives him the right to audaciously declare that he is a "judge of a Shari'ah court". We will mention some of the main points of agreement among the scholars with regards to what they have concurred are the conditions for a *Qādī*, there may be some points that we have not mentioned herein as we have only relayed the main aspects that the scholars mostly agree on.

الشرط الأول : البلوغ والعقل والحرية

MATURITY, INTELLIGENCE AND FREEDOM
The position of a *Qādī* necessitates that one be of mature mind and intellect and this cannot be attained except after puberty, this condition also negates insanity. Some of the *fuqahā* have also mentioned that:

ينبغي أن يكون من يتولى وظيفة القضاء صحيح الفكر ، جيد
الفطنة ، بعيداً عن السهو والغفلة يتوصل بذكائه إلى وضوح
المشكل وحل المعضل

The one who assumes the position of *Qādī* must be of sound mind, good expertise, distant from oversight and heedlessness. His

117

intelligence should lead to clarifying a problem and solving a difficulty.[132]

الشرط الثاني: الإسلام

ISLĀM

The *Qāḍī* must be a Muslim and it is not something a disbeliever can assume authority over, based on the saying of Allāh,

$$﴿وَلَن يَجْعَلَ اللَّهُ لِلْكَافِرِينَ عَلَى الْمُؤْمِنِينَ سَبِيلاً﴾$$

"...and never will Allāh give the disbelievers over the believers a way [to overcome them]."
{an-Nisā (4): 141}

The *Qāḍī* applies the rulings of the Divine Legislation and this requires precision and *īmān* in them before they are to be applied along with fear of Allāh.

الشرط الثالث: العدالة

INTEGRITY

Ibn Qudāmah mentions in *al-Mughnī*:

ولا يجوز تولية فاسق ولا من فيه نقص يمنع الشهادة

It is neither permissible for a fāsiq to assume the position of a Qāḍī nor one whose testimony is deficient.[133]

This is the view of the majority based on the saying of Allāh,

$$﴿يَا أَيُّهَا الَّذِينَ آمَنُوا إِن جَاءَكُمْ فَاسِقٌ بِنَبَإٍ فَتَبَيَّنُوا﴾$$

"O you who have believed, if there comes to you a disobedient one with information, investigate..."
{al-Hujurāt (49): 6}

الشرط الرابع: الاجتهاد

THE ABILITY TO MAKE IJTIHĀD

The scholars also make the condition that the *Qādī* is a *Mujtahid* this is the view of Imām Mālik, ash-Shāfi'ī, the *Hanābilah* and some of the *Ahnāf*. This is due to judgement demanding more precision than issuing *fatāwa* and even when issuing *fatāwā* the *Mufti* should not be a *Muqallid* (blind follower). They also use as a proof the *hadeeth* of Buraydah from the Messenger of Allāh (*sallallāhu 'alayhi wassallam*) that: *"There are three types of judges: one will be in Paradise and the other two in Hell. The one in Paradise is the one who knows the truth and judges according to it. As for the man who knows the truth but is unjust in his judgement, he will be in Hell. The man who judges between the people based on ignorance is also in Hell."*[134]

The conditions of *ijtihād* are: knowledge of the Book, the Sunnah, *ijmā'*, *ikhtilāf*, *qiyās* and Arabic language.[135] The scholars however have said that if there is a necessity it is permissible to follow a judge who is a *Muqallid* if there is not a *Mujtahid* present.

الشرط الخامس: الذكورة

BEING MALE

الشرط السادس : سلامة الحواس

HAVING SOUND SENSES

The *Qādī* has to have sound senses but the scholars have allowed one who is blind to be a *Qādī* based on the fact that Shu'ayb (*'alayhi-salām*) was blind and that a deaf person can communicate and understand sign-language.[136] Ibn Rushd summarises the conditions of a *Qādī* with the following:

أن يكون حراً مسلماً بالغاً ذكراً عاقلاً عدلاً

That he is free, Muslim, mature, male, intelligent and just.[137]

So we ask Choudary: at which Islāmic institute did you study for you to be bestowed with the honour of becoming a **"judge at a Shariah Court in the**

119

UK" and a "Principal Lecturer"? Not only is the so-called *London School of Shariah'* nothing but a re-hash of Omar Bakrī's cult followers but also there are no tangible premises to this place and no actual location!? Furthermore, Choudhary has no knowledge of the Arabic language! Hardly an endorsement therefore of him being any sort of "judge"! We first come across any mention of this "Shariah Court" by Omar Bakrī when, in a biography of him it stated: **"He is currently the judge of the Shari'ah court for the UK."**[138]

CHOUDHARY'S INTERVIEW WITH PRESS TV ON 20 MARCH 2009[139]

Fortunately for us, and unfortunately for Anjem Choudhary, we stumbled across a 20 minute interview that he conducted with Press TV on 20 March 2009. In this interview, we were privileged and pleased to hear a firsthand account of Anjem Choudhary's Islāmic credentials. According to Choudhary, his résumé includes the sciences of:

✓ *Ulūm -ul -Qur'ān,*
✓ *Usūl ul-Hadith* and
✓ *Usūl -ul- Fiqh.*

All studied for a period of 15 years, and all under the tutelage of his first in command, Omar Bakrī Muhammad. The initial conundrum that springs to mind is: how can we verify Choudhary's résumé when his teacher, himself is notorious for fabricating scholarly credentials? Since we have thoroughly exposed Bakrī's "DIY" (Do it yourself) homemade set of credentials, wouldn't this by default, at least cast a dubious shadow over Choudhary's credentials? Some may say, "No, this is not enough to pull the proverbial rug from under Choudhary's feet." However, our criticism of him and his dubitable credentials are not only contingent on this one single point.

A few weeks ago in the UK, Choudhary was a guest on BBC 1's Sunday morning discussion programme *The Big Questions.* During the show, (on which he publicly humiliated himself by indiscriminately denouncing everyone as a *kāfir* for opposing him), he was asked about Islām and its position regarding apostasy and tolerance. Feeling the need to first define the much mangled meaning of Islām, he decided to build his premise by giving the audience the root form from which the verbal noun 'Islām' stems from. This should have been a straight forward exercise in competence, which should of resulted in him giving the triliteral first pattern verb 'sa-li-ma', from which originates the fourth pattern verbal noun 'Islām', which is itself derived from the fourth form as-la-ma. However, Choudhary decided, right there and then, to re-write the rules of Arabic grammar, and absurdly declared that the verbal noun 'Islām' stems from the tenth pattern verb 'is-tas-la-ma'?! Some may claim that this may have been a mere slip of the tongue or that it is too much of a minute error to be raised. And granted that this may be true when isolated and debated as an independent point. But what about when you couple this rudimentary error with his audacious claims of studying the complex and profound sciences of Islām for a period of 15 years?! The glaring error which emanated from the jaws of Choudhary is that he substituted part of the definition of Islām for its linguistic root. It is true that part of the definition of Islām does mean Is-tis-lām (verbal noun form), but in no way is it derived from it. The aim here is not to publicly humiliate Choudhary on the basis of his rudimentary error. Rather, the aim here is to substantiate the shadow we cast over his credentials. How can a man, who has billed himself as "Judge of Sharee'ah Court of the UK" and has, allegedly, studied the sciences of Islām for 15 years, not have the capability to discern between the definition of Islām and its basic etymology?! Since Choudhary made this error, we had the opportunity to see Anjem Choudhary and he admitted, in front of witnesses in Brixton on Saturday 25th April 2009, that he erred. This therefore shows that his claims to have studied the deen are spurious at best.

If you scrutinize him carefully, one can clearly see that when he is discussing matters pertaining to legal or current affairs, he is a fish safely roaming his natural habitat. However, when he swims outside of his natural habitat, and starts to delve into principles of Islām, you can literally separate the two characters, which he has desperately tried to morph into one. Choudhary also has that manufactured, manicured voice which he developed during his days of serving the British legal System (as a lawyer). That voice provides him with a semblance of authority and shrouds him with a deceptive, thin layer of authenticity which conceals his lack of Islāmic knowledge.

Now we turn our attention, with concern, to Choudhary's excessive-compulsive *takfeer* disorder (ECTD). We clinically diagnosed him with such, because of the intrusive thoughts which constantly cause him to declare anyone or anything a *kāfir*. On three separate occasions, Choudary didn't conclude his discourse (or interview), except during it he made unrestricted *takfeer* of someone or of a Muslim organization such as the *MCB* or *MAB*. Before we investigate Choudhary's flagrant disregard, (and to some extent ignorance), of the cautionary principles which safe-guard a Muslim from harming himself, let us first remind ourselves of the perils of making unrestricted, knee-jerk *takfeer*. In the Two Saheehs from Ibn 'Umar *(radi Allāhu 'anhu)* who said: the Messenger of Allāh *(sallallāhu 'alayhi wassallam)* said:

روي ان رسول الله صلى الله عليه وسلم قال: إذا قال الرجل لصاحبه "يا كافر" فإنها تجب على أحدهما. فإن كان الذي قيل له كافر فهو كافر. وإلا رجع إليه ما قال.

"Whenever a man says to his brother: "O kāfir!" then it applies to one of them or it returns to the one who actually said it first."[140] In the Two Saheehs it is reported that the Messenger of Allāh *(sallallāhu 'alayhi wassallam)* said: *"Cursing a Muslim is sin and killing him is kufr."*[141] He also said *(sallallāhu 'alayhi wassallam)*: *"Whoever accuses a believer of kufr then it is as if he has killed him."*[142]

On the first part of Press TV after 4:23 (on youtube) Anjem Choudhary makes unequivocal and unrestricted *takfeer* of the *Muslim Council of Britain* (MCB) and the *Muslim Association of Britain* (MAB). So in the light of the authentic narrations, which warn the Muslims against shooting from the hip when it comes to the matter of *takfeer*, how can we not view Choudhary except as an arrogant, rash individual who has not only exposed himself to the threat mentioned in the Prophetic narrations but has also trivialized the words from where this threat is found.

Another ridiculous accusation, that begs to be refuted, is when Choudhary said: **"I think that the whole world today is governed by non-Islāmic law."**[143] Even in the most destitute of Muslim countries, we still find remnants of the *Sharee'ah*, albeit, distorted and contorted. The main point here is to refute the absolute manner in which he makes this redundant claim. This statement is a classical axiom, because its alleged truth is taken for granted, and then that which is taken for granted, serves as their (al-Muhajiroun's) starting point for many other absurd postulations. Thus, one postulation gives birth to another postulation until you have a whole spawn of illegitimate beliefs. On the basis of the above statement, it is not hard to understand how *al-Muhajiroun* find it easy to declare anyone or anything as a *kāfir*.

We also find that Choudhary stated, after 8:40 into an interview with Ian Collins on *Talksport Radio* in March 2009 (which can also be found Online), when asked about the *Sharee'ah* being implemented in Northern Nigeria and some controversies therein, Choudhary rejected this and said that Nigeria does not implement the *Sharee'ah*, even though there are parts of Northern Nigeria which do implement the *Sharee'ah*! So instead of objectively assessing cases of juristic errors and admitting this, Choudhary instead totally negates the existence of *Sharee'ah* implementation in Nigeria in order to gloss over juristic errors committed in areas where the *Sharee'ah* is implemented.

So what is the easiest and most effective way to demonstrate the folly of this audacious indictment (that the *Sharee'ah* is not implemented anyway in the Muslim world today), and thus, return it back to the realms of make believe from whence it came? We suppose the best way is to subject it to rigorous analyses by test-driving the durability of this statement on the tracks of the Saudi Legal system. The test is simple but highly effective. We will list just five laws which are functional in Saudi, and then we challenge anyone to eliminate just one by showing it to be incongruous with Islāmic Law:

Saudi Laws from Saudi Ministry of Justice	Islāmic basis of law
Inheritance Laws and the Determination of Heirs[144]	To document heirs and inheritance, the person tackling the issue should have full knowledge of the doctrine of inheritance because documenting eligible heirs needs to be made based on the knowledge of the rules of inheritance in the Islāmic *Sharee'ah* like textual shares and other rules of inheritance detailed in the books of jurisprudence. Some scholars have even singled out inheritance rules in special books for the fact that this science is so vast that it requires wide knowledge of its rulings. As for the method of documenting heirs as the only ones eligible to share the estate of the deceased person, the judge usually relies on testimonies. It suffices to have two witnesses who meet the legal conditions that qualify them to be witnesses. Their testimony should include mentioning the names of heirs, the reason of inheritance and negation

	of any information that no people other those mentioned by the witness are eligible to inheritance.
Awqāf (Endowment Laws)[145]	Allāh says, **"You will not attain piety until you spend of that which you love."** *{Āli 'Imrān (3): 92}* This verse clearly states that *waqf* is one of the forms of attainting piety. The evidence supporting this view is that as soon as Aboo Talhah *(radi Allāhu 'anhu)* heard this verse he rushed to endow the property best loved to him, namely his well-known date orchard known as al-Burayhā' which was located in a prime position near the Prophet's Mosque in Madeenah. The Prophet *(sallallāhu 'alayhi wassallam)* approved Aboo Talha's action to give it as *waqf* and also advised him as to its distribution i.e. to his relatives.[146] Ibn 'Umar *(radi Allāhu 'anhu)* narrated, "When 'Umar got a piece of land in Khaybar, he came to the Prophet (may Allāh's peace and blessings be upon him) and sad, 'I

have got a piece of land, better than which I have never got. So what do you advise me regarding it?' The Prophet said, 'If you wish you can keep it as an endowment to be used for charitable purposes.' So, 'Umar gave the land in charity (i.e. as an endowment) on the condition that the land would neither be sold nor given as a present, nor bequeathed, [and its yield] would be used for the poor, the kinsmen, the emancipation of slaves, *jihad*, and for guests and travellers; and its administrator could eat in a reasonable just manner [according to his labour], and he also could feed his friends without intending to be wealthy by its means.[147] Al-Qurtubī *(rahimahullāh)* writes:

> There is unanimous agreement amongst the Prophet's companions regarding the founding of endowments; for AbūBakr as-Siddeeq, 'Umar ibn al-Khattāb, 'Ali ibn Abī Tālib, 'Ā'ishah, Fātimah, 'Amr ibn al-

126

'Ās, Ibn az-Zubayr and Jābir all founded endowments, and their endowments in Makkah and Madeenah are well-known.[148]

Jābir ibn 'Abdullāh *(radi Allāhu 'anhu)* also said, "All the companion of the Prophet *(sallallāhu 'alayhi wassallam)* who had the means endowed [property]."[149]

Imām ash-Shāfi'ī *(rahimahullāh)* writes:

It has come to my attention that eighty companions of the Prophet (may Allāh's peace and blessings be upon him) from amongst the Ansār (helpers) had given *sadaqāt muharramāt* (inviolable charity).[150]

It is worth mentioning here that ash-Shāfi'ī calls endowments *sadaqāt muharramāt* (inviolable charity).[151]

At-Tirmidhī *(rahimahullāh)* also writes in this regard:

This was the practice of knowledgeable people from

	amongst the companions of the Prophet (may Allāh's peace and blessings be upon him) and others, and we do not know of any disagreement among the early scholars to the legality of endowing property and other assets.[152]
Rights of individuals regarding crimes that require hudood punishments[153]	Islām grants rights to those who are wrongly accused of crimes.
Alcoholic beverages and other intoxicants[154]	One of the definite Islāmic rulings which are by necessity known to every Muslim is the prohibition of wines and all types of intoxicants. In fact, proofs from the Qur'ān and the Prophetic traditions to this effect are numerous. These include the following: 1. Almighty Allāh says, **"O you who believe! Indeed, intoxicants, gambling, [sacrificing on] stone alters [to other than Allāh] and divining arrows are an abomination of the work of Satan, so avoid it that you may prosper. Satan only wants to excite enmity and hatred between**

you through intoxicants and gambling and to avert you from the remembrance of Allāh and from prayer; will you then desist?" {al-Mā'idah (5): 90-91}

2. He also says, "They ask you concerning wine and gambling, say, 'In them is great sin and some profit for people, but the sin is greater than the profit.'" {al-Baqarah (2): 219}

3. He also says, "He (i.e. the Prophet [may Allāh's peace and blessings be upon him) commands them what is just and forbids them what is evil; he allows them as lawful what is good [and pure] and prohibits them from what is bad [and impure]." {al-A'rāf (7): 157}

Muslim scholars are unanimously agreed that any kind of intoxicant, no matter its source, is strictly prohibited; they are also unanimously agreed that punishment is to be inflicted on anyone who becomes drunk of his own volition by using any kind of intoxicants and that 'khamr' (alcoholic beverage, wine, liquor) refers to any substance which causes intoxication, whether it is taken in small or large amounts.[155]

Ibn 'Umar *(radi Allāhu 'anhu)* narrated that Allāh's Messenger (may Allāh's peace and blessings be upon him) said, "Every intoxicant is *khamr* and every *khamr* is forbidden."[156]

Ibn 'Umar *(radi Allāhu 'anhu)* narrated that he heard [his father] 'Umar ibn al-Khattāb (may Allāh be pleased with him) say while delivering a sermon on the pulpit of Allāh's Messenger, 'O people, alcoholic drinks were prohibited by Divine Order, and these drinks are [normally] prepared from five things: grapes, dates, wheat, barley and honey. An alcoholic drink ('*kham*") is one that disturbs the mind.'[157]

Anas ibn Mālik *(radi Allāhu 'anhu)* said, "I was the cup-bearer of some people in the house of Abū Talhah on the day when alcohol was forbidden.

	Their alcohol had been prepared from dry dates or fresh dates when the announcer made the announcement.
	He (i.e. Abū Talhah) said to me, 'Go out and find out [what the announcement is]'. I went out [and found] an announcer making this announcement: 'Behold, alcohol has been declared unlawful.' He said: The liquor [was spilt and] flawed in the lanes of Madeenah. Abū Talhah said to me, 'Go out and spill it', and I did."[158]
The Ruling on litigants who are disrespectful or file false claims[159]	Muslim scholars have dealt with issues relating to such matters in such a way as to guarantee that those uncouth litigants are appropriately disciplined and that those who dare even think about being offensive and impolite are sufficiently warned.
	Allāh commands the faithful to observe justice in all matters. The Qur'ān says,
	"Indeed, Allāh enjoins justice and the doing of good to others; and giving

like kindred; and forbids indecency and manifest evil and wrongful transgression. He admonishes you that you may take heed."

{an-Nahl (16):9 }

He also commands them to administer justice when judging between people in their disputes, thus,

"Verily, Allāh commands you to make over the trusts to those entitled to them, and that when you judge between people you judge with justice."

{an-Nisā' (4): 58}

One of the requirements of justice which Almighty Allāh commands is that when someone files a false claim against somebody else, refuses to appear before the court when summoned without a valid reason or does appear before the court but demonstrates rudeness or disrespect towards his litigant, the judge or witnesses, he has to be appropriately punished for his bad manners and this punishment should serve the purpose of deterring others from doing the same thing. This punishment is bound to nip evil in the bud and preserve people's rights and safeguard their honour, among other things.

Abū Mulaikah narrated that two women were stitching shoes in a house or a room. Then one of them came out with an awl driven into her hand and she sued the other for it. The case was brought before Ibn 'Abbās. Ibn 'Abbās said, "Allāh's Messenger (peace and blessings be upon him) said, 'If people were to be given what they claim [without proving their claim] the life and property of the nation would be lost.' Will you remind her [i.e. the defendant] of Allāh and recite before her, **'Verily, those who sell the faith they owe to Allāh and their own solemn plighted word for a small price, they shall have no portion in the hereafter, nor will Allāh [deign to] speak to them or look at them on the Day of Judgement, nor will He** cleanse them [of sin]; and they shall have a grievous chastisement.' *{Āli 'Imrān (3): 77}*?" So they reminded her and she confessed. Ibn 'Abbās said, "The Prophet (peace and blessings be upon him) said, 'The oath is to be taken by the defendant [in absence of any proof against him].'"[160]

'Abdullāh ibn Mas'ood *(radi Allāhu 'anhu)* narrated that Allāh's messenger (peace and blessings be upon him) said, "Whoever takes an oath when asked to do so, in which he may deprive a Muslim of his property unlawfully, will meet Allāh, Who will be angry with him."[161]

'Abdullāh ibn 'Umar *(radi Allāhu 'anhu)* said, "I heard Allāh's Messenger *(sallallāhu 'alayhi wassallam)* say, '...And whoever disputes knowingly about something which is false, he remains in the displeasure of Allāh until he desists."[162]

'Abdullāh ibn 'Umar *(radi Allāhu 'anhu)* narrated that Allāh's Messenger (peace and blessing be upon him) said, "Whoever helps [someone] in a litigation unjustly will remain in the displeasure of Allāh until he desists."[163]

'Umar ibn Al-Khattāb *(radi Allāhu 'anhu)* sent a letter to Abū Mūsā al-Ash'arī, saying, "Adjudication is a firm religious obligation and a practice that must be upheld and followed... If a person claims a missing right or asserts that he is in possession of evidence, appoint a time-limit for him to reach. If he presents evidence, give him his right; otherwise decide against him, for this is most conducive to the dispelling of doubt and the removal of confusion..."[164]

Imām as-Sarakhsī, a famous Hanafi scholar, said regarding this report:

> His statement, 'decide against him' means 'oblige him to desist from harming people' and not to litigate without evidence.[165]

Commenting on the same report, Imām an-Nawawī writes:

This *hadeeth* is one of the important fundamentals of the rulings of the *Sharee'ah*. In fact, it states that no one's words are to be accepted for merely making a claim; rather he needs to produce evidence or the defendant's attestation. If he simply makes a claim and is thus given what he has claimed, some people will claim the fortunes and lives of other people, as the defendant cannot save his property and life, while a defendant can save them through evidence. This report is used as proof by the Shafii'ī School of jurisprudence and the majority of the past Muslim scholars to state that an oath is incumbent upon anyone against whom a claim has been filed, whether or not there is a dispute between him and the plaintiff.[166]

Just to eliminate a single one is an insurmountable task, because each of these laws is inherently Islām, and all have their roots firmly connected to the Qur'ān and the Sunnah. We have only provided five of a multitude of laws which are intrinsically Islāmic. Thus, for you viewing pleasure, we provide you with a link to the Saudi Ministry of Justice so that you, yourself can witness to what extent Saudi law is governed by *Sharee'ah*. Even the non-Muslims are aware that Saudi, to a large extent, is governed by Islāmic law. And we know this because they are constantly criticizing Saudi's 'barbaric' and 'medieval' polices and "human-rights violations". In particular, the death penalty and other parts of the penal system which remain faithful to Islāmic law. How can non-Muslims be aware of this basic fact, while the merry men of Bakrī remain oblivious?

One must wonder if he truly believes the words which string together his hyperbole. And after wondering about that, one must reason the real cause and motivation behind his need to deny the obvious and apparent. We firmly believe that this is all a product of their totalitarian mentality. Meaning, if anything of the *Sharee'ah* law system is missing, then this, (somehow), amounts to the complete absence of the *Sharee'ah* Law. Basically, their expectations and demands are all or nothing. It is as if they believe *Sharee'ah* law is a system of irreducible complexity, and that if a single part of it is missing, this causes the *Sharee'ah* system to effectively cease functioning. However, just a casual glance at the prophet's gradual methodology when establishing the *Sharee'ah* (over a period of 23 years), instantly dispels such nonsense. So the proposition unravels as follows: because it is alleged that Saudi fails to implement some of the *Sharee'ah* laws or it fails to implement it on all of its citizens, rich or poor, then it has failed in all of its endeavors to uphold Islāmic law. Indeed, it's a weird form deductive reasoning and logic, but what other way can one reason it?

Anjem Choudhary then goes on to say, **"Where do we exactly have Sharee'ah Law? If I was in Pakistan, I would be doing the same thing, if I was in Sudan, I would be doing the same thing."** We very much doubt he would be doing the same thing, and he should take a leaf out of Mājid Nawaz's book about what happens if you take liberties which are unconditionally given to you in liberal Western countries and then try to implement them in the Muslim countries! You never know, he may come back like Mājid and start spouting secular-liberal ideologies, which he himself was once an enemy of. We believe if the likes of Choudhary and his merry men went to a Muslim country and tried their antics and publicity stunts there, they would promptly learn why Islām outlaws all things which promote *khurūj*. Remind us, but wasn't that the case for Mājid?! Further to this, Choudhary constantly claims to represent the "Islāmic viewpoint" yet never ever gives the "Islāmic viewpoint" on rebellion, coups, revolutions and speaking out against the rulers. Again demonstrating Choudhary's scant knowledge of Islām and his political maneuvering in hiding Islāmic knowledge when it totally goes against his stance and views.

In the interview (after 3 minutes of Part 2 on *youtube*) Choudhary claims that it is permissible for a group of people to orchestrate a coup against the government. This exposes his blatant *Khāriji* and *Jihadi* characteristics and is another evidence to further the gap in terms of methodology between the Sunni-Salafis and *al-Muhajiroun*. From a historical and contemporary perspective, coups have rarely been a successful method for providing a better regime. Scour the annals of history and you will succumb to the fact that coups, in all of their manifestations, have had negative and detrimental effects on societies.

The question was presented to Choudary about the possible ways through which the *Sharee'ah* will come to the shores of the UK, Choudhary confidently responded by saying:

"...Or thirdly, there will be some people who will orchestrate a military coup to overthrow the regime, and give the security and authority to the Muslims, **as happened in Madeenah with the first Islamic state.**"

The above quote indicates to two things:

✓ Ignorance of the gradual Prophetic methodology which successively cultivated the path for the establishment of Islām as tangible legislative body.

✓ Ignorance surrounding the real definition of a *coup d'état* and its modern usage.

Firstly, we need to understand the gravity and far-reaching implications of this gross misleading statement. Here Choudary explicitly informs us that the *Sharee'ah* of Allāh was instituted on the back of a *coup d'état*. Implying that the only way Allāh could bring about the birth of Islām, as a legislative power, was by usurping the established Madinan authorities. We say this because coups are always a last desperate attempt to radically gain control of a country or state. So is this truly the way in which the Messenger of Allāh took Madeenah? Did Islām, with its numerous qualities and self evident truths, have to rely on such a desperate means to wrestle control away from the confederate tribes? The following narrations give us a clear picture of how Islām developed during the Madinan period. During the pilgrimage season in the eleventh year of Prophethood, the Prophet and a group of companions passed 'Aqabah in Mina. There they encountered six men from Yathrib (Madeenah), all who were of the tribe of Khazraj. When Allāh's Messenger met them, he asked:

"Who are you?"

"Of the tribe of Khazraj," they replied.

He asked them:

"Are you the allies of the Jews?"

They said, "Yes." He said:

"Then why not sit down for a little and I will speak to you."[167]

They sat with the Prophet, and the Prophet entertained their ears with the call of Islām. After a while, and after being totally convinced by the truthfulness and sincerity of Islām, they verbally embraced what their hearts had already accepted. Then they said to the Prophet, "We have left our community for no tribe is so divided by hate and enmity as they are. Allāh may cement our ties through you. **So, let us go and invite them to this religion of yours**; and if Allah unites them in it, no man will be dearer than you."[168]

The above highlighted words play an important role when refuting the neo-revolutionary claim of Choudhary. Nowhere in this text is there any mention of a plan to orchestrate a coup, neither in the words of the Messenger, nor in the words of the newly-converted of Madeenah, who apparently were content just to spread their new-found faith by word of mouth. It is said that this handful of Madinan men remained steadfast to their cause and succeeded in gaining support for Islam from among their fellow citizens. No word is mentioned about a conspiracy to orchestrate a coup.

The first pledge

The following year after the conversion of the six Madinan men, there came a group of people prepared to accept Islam. The group comprised five of the six men who had the previous year submitted. The non-Muslims of that group, right then bore witness to Allāh and His Messenger and verbally swore to uphold the duties of Islam. After the pledge was made, the Prophet sent Mus'ab bin 'Umayr al-'Abdirī to teach the residents of Madeenah the doctrines of Islām and to attempt to call to Islām those who still remained rigid to their polytheism. Through the endeavours of Mus'ab and the aid of Allāh, Islām spread from house to house like a bush fire in the midst of summer.

The following incident characterises the ease with which Islām conquers the hearts. One day Mus'ab and As'ad were on their way to the locality of Banī 'Abdul Ashhal and Banī Zafar, when they went into the premises of the latter clan. There they sat near a well conversing with some new converts. Sa'd bin Mu'adh and Usaid bin Hudayr, chiefs of the two clans heard of this meeting, so Usaid approached the Muslims armed with his spear while the other Sa'd excused himself on the grounds that As'ad was his maternal cousin. Husayd came closer cursing and swearing and accused the two men of fooling people weak of heart, and ordered that they stop it altogether. Mus'ab calmly invited him to sit saying, "If you are pleased with our talk, you can accept it; should you hold it as disgusting, you could freely immunise yourself against what you hate." "That is fair," said Usayd, pierced his lance in the sand, listened to Mus'ab and then heard some verses of the noble Qur'ān. His face beamed with satisfaction and pleasure before uttering any words of approval. He asked the two men about the procedures related to embracing Islam. They asked him to observe washing, cleanse his garment, bear witness to the truth and then perform a prayer of two units. He responded and did exactly what he was asked to do, and then said that there was a man (Sa'd bin Mu'adh) whose people would never hang back if he followed Islām. He then left to see Sa'd and his people. Sa'd could immediately understand that Husayd had changed. To a question posed by Sa'd, Husayd said that two men were ready to comply with whatever orders they received. He then arranged a meeting that provided the two men with a chance to talk privately. The previous scene with Husayd occurred again and Sa'd embraced Islām, and directly turned to his people **swearing that he would never talk with them until they believed in Allāh and Messenger.**[169]

So not only do we witness the ease with which Islām has in terms of entering the sincere hearts, but we also witness that there was no coup or uprising against the tribes of Madeenah during the period of Mus'ab's call. Leaders of tribes openly adopted Islām with pleasure and satisfaction and even refused to speak with their people until they entered the door of Islām, which is a far cry from the distorted picture which Choudhary attempts to sketch in people's minds.

There was no institutionalised form of sole-sovereign government amongst the Arabs in those days, as is found within modern political structures, for it to be said that the Companions made a coup. Furthermore, the method of a coup is in fact the exact insidious method which was utilised to depose the Companions *(radi Allāhu 'anhum)*. During the later years of the Caliphate of 'Uthmān *(radi Allāh 'anhu)*, an underground conspiracy was hatched, led by Abdullāh Ibn Saba, who had outwardly converted to Islam, in order to produce political unrest. The conspiracy succeeded, mainly because a lack of proper communication facilities in those days made the spread of rumors against the Khaleefah rather easy. This resulted in a rebellion against 'Uthman *(radi Allāhu 'anhu)* on various fabricated charges of nepotism, and he was martyred in the course of the rebellion. In this chaotic situation, 'Ali *(radi Allāhu 'anhu)* became the next Caliph. A *coup d'etat* therefore can never produce a stable and positive change as it does not involve changing the beliefs and views of the people. Instead, we need to follow the example of the Prophet Muhammad *(sallallāhu 'alayhi wassallam)*, and therefore teaching, preaching, exhortation and purification of souls are essential initial steps in the establishment of Khilāfah. We also believe that there is a severe deficiency in the level and depth of *īmān* among the Muslims, and the Islamic revival cannot be realized without the revival of true *īmān* in a significant portion of the Muslim society via the Book and Sunnah in totality at all levels.

The military historian and advisor to the Reagan Administration Edward Luttwak stated in his landmark book *Coup d'État: a Practical Handbook* (Cambridge, MA: Harvard University Press, 1979) says:

A coup consists of the infiltration of a small, but critical, segment of the state apparatus, which is then used to displace the government from its control of the remainder...[170]

Choudhary's promotion of an insidious *coup d'État* also reveals that he will even utilize methods which oppose the Prophetic methodology in order to bring about change and a *coup d'État* as we have seen is a strategy that is promoted by non-Muslim agencies in order to shape their hegemony around the world. Strategically, a coup usually involves control of some active portion of the military while neutralizing the remainder of a country's armed services. This active group captures or expels leaders, seizes physical control of important government offices, means of communication, and the physical infrastructure, such as streets and power plants. As a side note, it is uncanny how all neo-*Khawārij* groups have a joint obsession for fast-track revolutionary methods for social and political reform, who then always attempt to artificially inseminate their false doctrines and methods into the sources and history of Islām. This just reinforces the notorious characteristic of the people of innovation, and that is to formulate false principles and then scavenge the sources to try and justify them.

Finally, the reformed and revised position of Choudhary on the rulings of the Muslim who resides in non-Muslim lands, as exhibited in the interview, ever-more strengthens the religio-political evolution which has been dynamic since the illegitimate birth of the cult following of OBM.

«4»
STATEMENTS OF SCHOLARS ABOUT REVOLTING AGAINST A MUSLIM RULER

Shaykh 'AbdulLateef bin 'AbdurRahmān bin Hasan Āl ush-Shaykh stated in *ad-Durur as-Sunniyyah fī Ajwibatin-Najdiyyah*,[171] vol.7, pp.177-78:

وأضرب لك مثلاً بالحجاج بن يوسف الثقفي، وقد اشتهر أمره في الأمة بالظلم والغشم والإسراف في سفك الدماء وانتهاك حرمات الله، وقتل من قتل من سادات الأمة: كـ"سعيد بن جبير" وحاصر ابن الزبير وقد عاذ بالحرم الشريف، واستباح الحرمة، وقتل ابن الزبير –مع أن ابن الزبير قد أعطاه الطاعة وبايعه عامة أهل مكة والمدينة واليمن وأكثر سواد العراق، والحجاج نائب عن مروان...ولم يعهد أحد من الخلفاء إلى مروان، ولم يبايعه أهل الحل والعقد–**ومع ذلك لم يتوقف أحد من أهل العلم في طاعته** **والانقياد له فيما تسوغ طاعته فيه من أركان الإسلام وواجباته.**

وكان ابن عمر –رضي الله تعالى عنهما–ومن أدرك الحجاج من أصحاب رسول الله –صلى الله تعالى عليه وآله وسلم–لا ينازعونه ولا يمتنعون من طاعته فيما يقوم به الإسلام، ويكمل به الإيمان.

وكذلك في زمن التابعين، كـ: ابن المسيب، والحسن البصري، وابن سيرين، وإبراهيم التيمي، وأشباههم ونظرائهم من سادات الأمة.

واستمر العمل على هذا بين علماء الأمة من سادات الأمة وأئمتها، يأمرون بطاعة الله ورسوله، والجهاد في سبيله مع كل إمام بر أو فاجر، كما هو معروف في كتب أصول الدين والعقائد

وكذلك بنو العباس: استولوا على بلاد المسلمين قهراً بالسيف، لم يساعدهم أحد من أهل العلم والدين، وقتلوا خلقاً كثيراً، وجماً غفيراً من بني أمية وأمرائهم ونوابهم، وقتلوا ابن هبيرة أمير العراق، وقتلوا الخليفة مروان، حتى نقل أن السفاح قتل في يوم واحد نحو الثمانين من بني أمية، ووضع الفرش على جثثهم، وجلس عليها، ودعا بالمطاعم والمشارب!!! ومع ذلك فسيرة الأئمة كـ: الأوزاعي، ومالك، والزهري، والليث بن سعد، وعطاء بن أبي رباح مع هؤلاء الملوك لا تخفى على من له مشاركة في العلم واطلاع .

والطبقة الثانية من أهل العلم، كـ: أحمد، ومحمد بن إسماعيل، ومحمد بن إدريس، وأحمد بن نوح، وإسحاق بن راهويه، وإخوانهم...وقع في عصرهم من الملوك ما وقع من البدع العظام، وإنكار الصفات، ودعوا إلى ذلك، وامتحنوا فيه، وقتل من قتل، كـ: أحمد بن نصر، ومع ذلك فلا يعلم أن أحداً منهم نزع يداً من طاعة، ولا رأى الخروج عليهم..."أهـ

A similitude can be put to you with al-Hajjāj bin Yūsuf ath-Thaqafī and he became famous in the Ummah for his oppression, suppression, excess in blood-shed and dishonouring the sanctities of Allāh and killing whoever he wanted from the notables of the Ummah: such as Sa'eed bin Jubayr and besieging Ibn az-Zubayr even though he had sought refuge in the Haram, Hajjāj made lawful the sanctified and killed Ibn az-Zubayr. Even though Ibn az-Zubayr had pledged obedience to him along with the people of Makkah, Madeenah, al-Yemen and the majority of al-'Irāq. Hajjāj was the deputy of Marwān, but neither did any of the Khulafā' nor any of the influential people in authority pledge allegiance to Marwān. Yet with this, none of the people of knowledge withheld from obedience to him and complying with him in those matters where obedience is

144

allowed from the pillars of Islām and its obligations. Ibn 'Umar *(radi Allāhu 'anhuma)* and those present from the Companions of the Prophet *(sallallāhu alayhi wassallam)* at the time did not challenge him or prevent anyone from obeying him in those things which Islām instructs and perfect eemān. It was likewise during the time of Hajjāj for the Successors (Tābi'een) like: Ibn ul-Musayyib, al-Hasan al-Basrī, Ibn Seereen, Ibrāheem at-Taymī and their likes from the illustrious people of the Ummah. This way continued among the leading scholars of the Ummah who instructed obedience to Allāh and His Messenger, and jihād in the way of Allāh with every leader whether righteous or sinful as is well-known in the books of Usūl ud-Deen (Religious Principles) and 'Aqā'id (Creed). And likewise during the epoch of Banu 'Abbās (the Abbasids), for they gained ascendancy over the Muslim lands via the sword, and none of the people of knowledge and *deen* helped them in this, and they killed many from creation such as killing a large amount of the Bani Umayyah (Umayyads) and their leaders and deputies. They killed Ibn Hubayrah, the leader of 'Irāq and they killed the Khaleefah Marwān, to the extent that it has been transmitted that they killed around 80 members of Banu Umayyah in just one day and they laid a blanket over their corpses and sat on them calling for food and drink!!! Yet with all of this, the way of the Imāms of the time such as: al-Awzā'ī, Mālik, az-Zuhrī, al-Layth ibn Sa'd, 'Atā' bin Abee Rabāh with those kings is not hidden from anyone who has any share of knowledge and awareness. The third stage of scholars included: Ahmad, Muhammad bin Ismā'īl, Muhammad bin Idrees, Ahmad bin Nūh, Ishāq bin Rāhawayh and their brothers, and during their time were kings with major innovations, such as denying the Attributes of Allāh and calling to that and they (the scholars from the People of *Sunnah*) were put to the test in this regard. And whomsoever was killed during this era such as Ahmad bin Nasr, yet with all of this it is not known that any of them removed the hand of obedience and did not view that khurooj (rebellion) should be made against those leaders.

Shaykh ul-Islām Ibn Taymiyyah *(rahimahullāh)* stated in the fifth volume of *Minhāj us-Sunnah* on page 112:

وكذلك النجاشي هو وإن كان ملك النصارى فلم يطعه قومه في الدخول

في الإسلام بل إنما دخل معه نفر منهم ولهذا لما مات لم يكن هناك من يصلي

عليه فصلى عليه النبي صلى الله عليه وسلم بالمدينة خرج بالمسلمين إلى

المصلى فصفهم صفوفا وصلى عليه وأخبرهم بموته .يوم مات وقال إن أخا

لكم صالحا من أهل الحبشة مات وكثير من شرائع الإسلام أو أكثرها لم

يكن دخل فيها لعجزه عن ذلك فلم يهاجر ولم يجاهد ولا حج البيت بل قد

روى أنه لم يكن يصلي الصلوات الخمس ولا يصوم شهر رمضان ولا يؤدي

الزكاة الشرعية لأن ذلك كان يظهر عند قومه فينكرونه عليه وهو لا يمكنه

مخالفتهم

And likewise an-Najāshi who was a Christian king of his country would not have been obeyed by the people whom he ruled over in accepting Islām and only a few people accepted Islām with him. For this reason, when he died there were no Muslims to pray over him in his country. The Prophet (sallallāhu 'alayhi wassallam) in Madeenah prayed over Najāshi, the people went out to a musalla and arranged rows in order to pray the janazah for an-Najāshi and the Prophet (sallallāhu 'alayhi wassallam) prayed over him.[172] He then informed them that an-Najāshi had died saying "Indeed, your righteous brother from the people of Habasha (Ethiopia) died today." Many of the symbols and institutions of Islām, or most of them, were not established in Habasha due to his (an-Najāshi's) inability to implement them there. He did not make hijra, he did not make jihād, he did not make Hajj, indeed it is even stated that he did not even pray the five daily prayers, fast or give the Divinely Legislated Zakat! Because if all of that was made apparent to his people and they saw all of that and that he was doing all of that they would have rejected him and objected, and thus it would not have been possible for him to have opposed them.

Shaykh 'Ali Hasan al-Halabī al-Atharī stated about this:

146

This is a very precise point as an-Najāshi therefore was aware of many of the symbols and institutions of Islām and knew about them yet was unable to implement and apply them. I stopped and appended some notes at this point here as some people confuse the story of an-Najāshi wherein it is stated that an-Najāshi had not been made aware of the regulations of the Divine Legislation and did not know about any of the symbols and institutions of the Divine Legislation, but this is clear in the text from Shaykh ul-Islām who stated: '**Many of the symbols of Islām, or most of them, were not established in Habasha due to his (an-Najāshi's) inability to implement them there.**'[173]

Shaykh ul-Islām Ibn Taymiyyah continues:

ونحن نعلم قطعا أنه لم يكن يمكنه أن يحكم بينهم بحكم القرآن

والله قد فرض على نبيه بالمدينة أنه إذا جاءه أهل الكتاب لم يحكم بينهم إلا

بما أنزل الله إليه وحذره أن يفتنوه عن بعض ما أنزل الله إليه وهذا مثل

الحكم في الزنا للمحصن بحد الرجم وفي الديات بالعدل والتسوية في الدماء

بين الشريف والوضيع النفس بالنفس والعين بالعين وغير ذلك

والنجاشي ما كان يمكنه أن يحكم بحكم القرآن فإن قومه لا يقرونه على

ذلك

We know absolutely that it was not possible for him to rule amongst his people with the Qur'ān[174] and Allāh obligated His Messenger in Madeenah that if the People of the Book come to him he should not judge between them except with what Allāh had revealed and warned him from the fact that the People of the Book swerve him away from some of what Allāh has revealed. For example, the punishment and ruling upon zinā, blood-money, the recompense for killing another soul, an eye for an eye etc. So an-Najāshi was not able to rule with the rule of the Qur'ān as his people would not have accepted that.

Shaykh ul-Islām Ibn Taymiyyah mentions all of this in regards to dealings between Muslims and Mongols wherein a Muslim is not able to implement the Sharee'ah in totality due to the Mongols preventing this and threatening the Muslims against this. Shaykh 'Ali Hasan therefore highlights:

We can say now, and I do not intend to make it easy or to make excuses without right however we are speaking about the reality which is that most of the rulers in this era, if not all of them unfortunately from the Muslims, not to mention the non-Muslims, rule for the sake of a greater state! They are not able to behave and are not able to do anything which opposes them (that greater state). Therefore, they neither reject Islām nor reject the rule of Islām, rather they rule according to some of the regulations of Islām and all praise is due to Allāh. As *masājid* are widespread, the institution of the month of *Ramadān* is widespread and we see that there is stern opposition if one breaks the fast to eat and the restaurants are all closed during the daytime in *Ramadān*, therefore the main symbols and institutions of Islām are clearly apparent and present. We see that the institution of *Hajj* has a great importance in all of the Muslim countries along with establishing support for people who make *Hajj*. We also see the collection boxes for *Zakat* even if it is made obligatory upon the people strictly by these Muslims countries, it is still coordinated, arranged and organised along with exhortation to pay it. Indeed, in some Muslim countries they want to make it obligatory to give *Zakat*. All of this indicates that the main symbols and institutions of Islām are apparent and are present along with importance attached to Islām, but do they apply all of Islām? So they fall into the same as that an-Najāshi did before them. They (the leaders) are not able to rule totally according to what Allāh has revealed because their people do not agree with that. As the greater states, the hypocrites and the people who do not want the Divine Legislation of Allāh - do not agree with their leaders in this and doing it would lead to tribulations and dangerous affairs. We do not say all of this out of defending them, making light of the matter or out of making light of their condition, rather we make this clear in order for the Divinely Legislated ruling on the issue to be clear. So to make *takfeer* of such leaders is not permissible along with the excuses which we have just mentioned and Allāh knows best.

So if all of these regulations have been verified in theory and practice, and the narrations regarding an-Najāshi *(radi Allāhu 'anhu)* are apparent as the correct foundation of this issue then we must go to another important related issue. It is an issue which the opposers try to utilise, as they try to utilise the other issue yet without really taking full account of either of them, and it is the issue of revolting against the rulers. Most of those who make *takfeer* of the Muslim rulers are the very same people who revolt against the Muslim rulers, incite and rouse the people against the leaders and talk about them so as to destabilise the trust, security and *eemān* of the *ummah*. Few of them seek to ascertain if such a ruler may be a sinner and thus revolting against him is deemed permissible as those who seek this type of research in reality are not the people to debate with as they are few in these times. Rather, those who have become popularised during this era are those who make *takfeer* of the leaders and legitimise revolting against them based upon making *takfeer* of them. Revolting against the Muslim rulers is an affair which according to the consensus of the *ummah* is not permissible and we will speak initially about the Muslim rulers who oppose the Divine Legislation in a small portion, or a large portion, yet they are still within the fold of Islām as they have not expelled themselves from the religion and they have not become *kuffār* due to what they have done or due to actions that they have committed. The texts from the scholars regarding this issue are plentiful and very abundant, I will highlight some of it which is stronger than if it comes merely from my own self, as if statements emerge from the scholars they are stronger proofs and evidences and especially if there is a consensus (of the Muslim scholars) mentioned within them.

'Aqeedah on Dealing with the Rulers from Imām Abū Bakr al-Ismā'īlī (d. 371 AH):

Before we come to the relevant text from Abū Bakr al-Ismā'īlī's *I'tiqād Ahl us-Sunnah* we will look at his biography. Al-Hasan bin 'Ali al-Hāfidh stated in *Tāreekh Jurjān*[175]:

> Shaykh Abū Bakr should have classified his own Sunan as he was able to write much due to his knowledge, understanding and honour.

Abū 'Abdullāh al-Hākim stated, as reported in *Siyar 'A'lām un-Nubalā*, vol.16, p.294:

> Al-Ismā'īlī was one of his time, a Shaykh of the Muhadditheen and Fuquhā and the most noble of them in leadership....there is no difference among the scholars of the two sciences and their intelligentsia about Abū Bakr.

Adh-Dhahabī stated in *Siyar*, vol.16, p.292: "**the Imām, Hāfidh, Hujjah, Faqeeh, Shaykh ul-Islām.**" As-Subkī stated in *Tabaqāt ash-Shāfi'iyyah al-Kubrā*, vol.3, p.7: "**The Imām of the people of Jurjān,**[176] **the reference point in Fiqh and Hadeeth, the author of classifications.**"

His Birth, Life and Death:

He is the Imām, Hāfidh, Hujjah, Faqeeh, Shaykh ul-Islām Abū Bakr ibn Ibrāheem bitn Ismā'īl bin al-'Abbās al-Jurjānī al-Ismā'īlī ash-Shāfi'ī the author of *as-Saheeh* and the Shaykh of the Shāfi'iyyah, he was born in 277 AH/890 CE. He wrote down hadeeth with his own handwriting while he was young and started seeking knowledge in 289 AH. He classified narrations which bore witness to his leadership in *fiqh* and *hadeeth*. Hamza stated "**Abū Bakr died in Ghazzah in Rajab 371 AH/June 902 CE aged 94 years of age.**"

His Works:

Dr. Ziyad Muhammad Mansūr mentioned in *Kitāb ul-Mu'jam fī Asāmī Shuyūkh Abī Bakr al-Ismā'īlī* (al-Madeenah al-Munawarrah: Maktabah al-'Ulūm wa'l-Hikam, 1410 AH/1990 CE, First Edn.)[177] 17 works:

1. *al-Mu'jam fī Asāmī Shuyūkhihi*
2. *al-Mustakhraj 'alā Saheeh il-Bukhārī*

3. *al-Madkhal ilā Saheeh il-Bukhārī*, with objections and answers to them.[178]
4. *al-Musnad al-Kabeer*
5. *Musnad 'Umar*
6. *Musnad 'Ali*
7. *Musnad Yahyā al-Ansārī*
8. *Hadeeth Yahyā bin Abī Bakr.*
9. *al-Fawā'id*
10. *al-'Awālī*
11. *Kitāb Ahādeeth il-'A'mash*
12. *Hadeeth*, which has the *ahādeeth* of other *hadeeth* scholars, *al-Majmū'* 31.
13. *Su'alāt us-Sahmī*
14. *Mu'jam us-Sahābah*
15. *Su'alāt ul-Barqānī*
16. *Risālah fi'l'Aqeedah*, this was mentioned by as-Sābūnī[179] and Ibn Taymiyyah.[180]
17. *Kitāb fi'l-Fiqh*
18. *Kitāb 'I'tiqād Ahl us-Sunnah*
19. *Jamu' Hadeeth Mis'ar*,[181] this was mentioned by Ibn Rajab al-Hanbalī.[182]

His 'Aqeedah:

Al-Hāfidh Abū Bakr al-Ismā'īlī had *Salafi* beliefs in accordance with the way of the *Ahl ul-Hadeeth wa'l-Athar*. For this reason, Ibn Katheer stated: "He compiled books then benefitted and refined, and he mastered criticism and creed."[183]

This makes clear three matters:

❖   That he has a book entitled *'I'tiqād Ahl us-Sunnah*

❖   His statements regarding *'aqeedah* which have been transmitted by many Imāms of this issue.

❖   His treatise on *'aqeedah* which was sent to the people of Jeelān.

Al-Hāfidh Abū 'Uthmān Ismā'eel bin 'AbdurRahmān as-Sābūnī stated in *'Aqeedah Salaf wa Ashāb ul-Hadeeth*, p.27:

I read in the treatise of Shaykh Abū Bakr al-Ismā'īlī to the people of Jeelān that he said 'Indeed, Allāh descends to the Heavens of the

Dunya in accordance with the most correct understanding from the Messenger of Allāh *(sallallāhu alayhi wassallam)*...'

Abū 'Uthmān as-Sābūnī also transmitted the following from al-Ismā'īlī: As for the wording and recitation *(Lafdh)* of the Qur'ān then Shaykh Abī Bakr al-Ismā'īlī *(rahimahullāh)* mentioned in his treatise that he classified to the people of Jeelān that: 'Whoever claims that his recitation of the Qur'ān is created intending the Qur'ān has spoken with the speech of those who say the Qur'ān is created.'

His Biographical Sources

❖ *Tāreekh Jurjān* [The History of Gorgan], pp.108-116, no.98
❖ *Al-Kāmil fī't-Tāreekh*, pp.9, 16
❖ *Al-Muktasar fī Akhbār il-Bashr*, vol.2, p.122
❖ *Tāreekh Ibn al-Waradī*, vol.1, p.305
❖ *Al-Muntadham*, vol.7, p.108, no.144
❖ *Tadhdhkirat ul-Huffādh*, vol.3, p.947, no.897
❖ *Al-Ansāb*, vol.1, 'lām' ,36, 'alif'
❖ *Al-'Ibar*, vol.2, p.358
❖ *Tabaqāt ush-Shāfi'iyyah al-Kubrā*, vol.2, 80
❖ *Shadharāt udh-Dhahab*, vol.3, p.75
❖ *Al-Bidāyah wa'n-Nihāyah*, vol.11, p.298
❖ *Marāt ul-Janān*, vol.2, p.396
❖ *Tabaqāt ul-Huffādh*, pp.381-2
❖ *Duwal ul-Islām*, vol.1, p.229
❖ *Tabaqāt ul-Fuquhā* by Shirāzī, pp.116, 121
❖ *Tabaqāt ush-Shāfi'iyyah* by Ibn Hidāyatillāh, p.95
❖ *Wafayāt ul-'A'yān*, vol.3, p.168
❖ *Al-Wāfee bi'l-Wafayāt*, vol.6, p.213, no.2678
❖ *Tabyeen Kadhib al-Muftarī*, p.192
❖ *Mu'jam ul-Buldān*, vol.2, p.122
❖ *Tabaqāt ul-'Abbādī*, p.86
❖ *Al-Lubāb*, vol.1, p.58
❖ *As-Siyar*, vol.16, pp.292-96
❖ *Al-'I'lān bi't-Tawbeekh*, p.141
❖ *Kashf udh-Dhunoon*, p.1735
❖ *Al-'A'lām*, vol.1, p.83

- ❖ *Hidāyat ul-'Ārifeen*, vol.1, p.66
- ❖ *Mu'jam ul-Mu'allifeen*, vol.1, p.135
- ❖ *Tāreekh ut-Turāth al-'Arabī*, vol.1, p.329

Tracing the Book 'I'tiqād Ahl us-Sunnah to Abū Bakr al-Ismā'īlī:

The creed of al-Ismā'īlī was affirmed by Ibn Qudāmah[184] where he said: ...ash-Shareef Abu'l-'Abbās Mas'ood bin 'AbdulWāhid bin Matr al-Hāshimī informed us[185] saying: al-Hāfidh Abu'l-'Ulā Sā'id bin Sayyār al-Harawī informed us saying: Abu'l-Hasan 'Ali bin Muhammad al-Jurjānī informed us saying: Abu'l-Qāsim Hamzah bin Yūsuf as-Sahmī informed us saying: Abū Bakr Ahmad bin Ibrāheem al-Ismā'īlī informed us in his book *'I'tiqād Ahl us-Sunnah* saying: 'Know, may Allāh have mercy on us and you, that the madhdhab of the people of hadeeth, the people of *Sunnah wa'l-Jama'ah,* is...'

Via Ibn Qudāmah and transmitted by adh-Dhahabī[186] who said: "Ismā'eel ibn 'AbdurRahmān bin al-Farā' informed us: Shaykh Muwaffaquddeen 'Abdullāh..." *al-'Allāmah* al-Albānī[187] stated about this *isnād*: "All of the men in the *isnād* are trustworthy and well-known except for Mas'ood bin 'AbdulWāhid al-Hāshimī, I did not find a biography of him." Adh-Dhahabī mentioned the accuracy of this *isnād* saying in his book *al-Arba'een*: "We heard this creed with an authentic *isnād* from him (meaning: from al-Ismā'īlī)."[188] Ibn Taymiyyah stated in *Dar' at-Ta'ārud*:

> The statements which do not have any basis in the Book, *Sunnah* and *Ijmā'* are the negated statements which are stated by the *Jahmiyyah*, *Mu'tazilah* and others. They describe the people who affirm the Attributes mentioned in the confirmed texts who say "the Qur'ān is not created or that Allāh will be seen in the Hereafter or that Allāh is Above the Worlds", as being *"Mujassima"* (anthropomorphists) and *"Hashwiyyah"* (worthless ones). Yet these three matters have been agreed upon by the *Salaf* of the *Ummah* and its Imāms. The *ijmā* of *Ahl us-Sunnah* from the statements of the *Salaf* in these matters has been corroborated by more than one of the Imāms, such as: Ahmad bin Hanbal, 'Ali bin al-Madanī, Ishāq bin Ibrāheem, Dāwūd bin 'Ali...**and like Abū Bakr al-Ismā'īlī...**"[189]

Al-Hāfidh Ibn Hajar al-'Asqalānī stated in *Fath ul-Bārī*, transmitting from al-Ismā'īlī what is connected to the division between *īmān* and Islām: "Al-

153

Ismāʻīlī relayed this from the people of *Sunnah wa'l-Jama'ah* who said 'They are both different in their evidences when compared...'[190]

In his *'I'tiqād Ahl us-Sunnah*, Imām Abū Bakr al-Ismāʻīlī states in point no.43:

": ...ويرون الصلاة-الجمعة وغيرها-خلف كل إمام مسلم، براً كان أو

فاجراً، فإن الله-عزّ وجلّ-فرض الجمعة وأمر بإتيانها فرضاً مطلقاً مع

علمه تعالى بأن القائمين يكون منهم الفاجر والفاسق، فلم يستثن وقتاً

دون وقت، ولا أمراً بالنداء للجمعة دون أمر، ويرون جهاد الكفار

معهم، وإن كانوا جورة، ويرون الدعاء لهم بالإصلاح والعطف إلى

العدل، ولا يرون الخروج بالسيف عليهم، ولا القتال في الفتنة، ويرون

الدار دار إسلام لا دار كفر-كما رأته المعتزلة-ما دام النداء بالصلاة

والإقامة بها ظاهرين، وأهلها ممكنين منها آمنين""اعتقاد أهل

السنة"للإسماعيلي ص(50-51) والنقل عن"النقول الواضحة..."ص(23)

They (*Ahl us-Sunnah*) view that the prayer, whether it is congregational or any other, should be made behind every Muslim Imām, good or sinful, because Allāh made the congregational prayer obligatory specifically and absolutely. This is even though Allāh knew that some of those who establish it will be immoral and sinful, and he did not exempt any time or instruct to make another congregation.

Then he states:

44 – They view *jihād* against the *kuffār* with the leaders even if the leaders are sinful and immoral.

45 – They view that du'ā should be made for the leaders so that they be righteous and just.

46 – They do not view that khurooj be made against the leaders with the sword (i.e. with weapons).

47 – Nor should there be any fighting during fitna (tribulations).

48 – They view that the transgressing group be fought against with the just Imām.

154

49 – They view that the abodes are places of Islām (Dār ul-Islām) and not Dār ul-Kufr as the Mu'tazilah say. As long as the call to prayer is made and the prayer established apparently and the people are established (with their deen) in it with safety.[191]

Imām Abū Ja'far at-Tahāwī, author of 'Aqeedah Tahāwiyyah, which was explained by Ibn Abi'l-'Izz al-Hanafī, states:

"ولا نرى الخروج على أئمتنا وولاة أمورنا وإن جاروا ولا ندعوا عليهم، ولا ننزع يداً من طاعة، ونرى طاعتهم في طاعة الله عز وجل فريضة ما لم يأمروا بمعصية، وندعو لهم بالصلاح والمعافاة" شرح الطحاوية"ص(371)

We do not view (that it is permissible to) revolt against our leaders or those who are responsible for our affairs and even if they transgress we do not make du'ā against them[192] and we do not take back the covenant of obedience from them[193] and we view that obedience to them is from obedience to Allāh and obligatory[194] as long as they do not command to disobedience and we make du'ā to Allāh for them to have correctness and good health.[195]

As for the consensus which indicates this clearly is that which was stated by Imām an-Nawawī (rahimahullāh) in his explanation of Saheeh Muslim wherein he stated:

وأما الخروج عليهم وقتالهم فحرام بإجماع المسلمين وإن كانوا فسقة ظالمين

As for revolting against the rulers and leaders and fighting against them then it is harām (impermissible) according to the consensus of the Muslims even if they are sinful transgressors.[196]

Al-Hāfidh Ibn Hajar al-'Asqalānī transmitted this in his book Fath al-Bārī vol.13, p.7) from Imām Ibn Battāl, who has an explanation of Saheeh Bukhārī which has been published:

ونقل الحافظ ابن حجر -رحمه الله -الإجماع على عدم جواز الخروج على السلطان الظالم: فقال قال ابن بطال:"وفي الحديث حجة على ترك الخروج على السلطان ولو جار، وقد أجمع الفقهاء على وجوب طاعة

155

السلطان المتغلب والجهاد معه، وأن طاعته خير من الخروج عليه لما في

ذلك من حقن الدماء وتسكين الدهماء"فتح الباري)13/7(

The fuquhā (Islāmic jurists) have reached consensus that obedience
must be made to the leader who becomes dominant (mutaghallib)[197]
and making jihād with him and that obeying him is better than
revolting against him due to the blood which would be spilt in that
and this would not be permissible unless there was clear kufr from
the leader.[198]

Shaykh 'Ali Hasan al-Halabī al-Atharī notes:

Some people have thrown doubt upon this foundation which we
have mentioned and they have tried to refute it due to some events
that took place at the dawn of Islāmic history which stemmed from
the tribulations which took place between the companions of the
Prophet *(radi Allāh 'anhum)*. They thus use as a proof against the
consensus the examples of al-Husayn, 'Abdullāh ibn Zubayr, and
those who were with them from the people of Madeenah in revolting
against Banee 'Umayyah. This was at the beginnings of Islāmic
history when the companions were still present. There are two
aspects to refute this doubt:

1.   All of this stemmed from the tribulation which took place
among the companions *(radi Allāhu 'anhum)* about whom the
Messenger of Allāh said: *"If my companions are mentioned then be silent"*
so it is not permissible to use as an evidence an issue which was a
tribulation which is prohibited to enter, use as an evidence or even
discuss. This is evidence in itself and it opposes the text, opposes any
benefit and opposes the general evidences from the Divine
Legislation.

2.   The second thing is that many of the people of knowledge noted
that this disagreement took place in the beginning however the
consensus which was later established opposed it (revolt). The
statement from Imām an-Nawawī wherein he stated: **'This difference
was in the beginning and then the consensus developed that
prevented revolting against the Muslim leaders.'**[199] There are other
statements such as that in *at-Tahdeeb wa't-Tahdheeb* of al-Hāfidh Ibn
Hajar al-'Asqalānī who mentioned in whilst highlighting the

156

biography of al-Hasan ibn Sālih ibn Hayy. He noted: **'This was in the affair in the past at the beginning of Islām and then the ummah agreed upon the opposite.'**

As for the evidence for the consensus then a consensus cannot be verified except with evidences, so what are the evidences for this consensus which are used by many of the people of knowledge? As we said from it (the evidences) are the statements from an-Nawawee, Ibn Battāl, al-Hāfidh ibn Hajar and other people of knowledge. The evidences are abundant and we will highlight the most important evidences. From the evidences are the *hadeeth* of 'Ubādah ibn Sāmit which is in *Saheeh Muslim* wherein the Prophet *(sallallāhu alayhi wassallam)* stated: "We pledged allegiance[200] to the Messenger of Allāh that we hear and obey and in what we love and what we hate and in what is hard for us and what is not hard for us and even in things which we do not like and not that we should not dispute over leadership and not try to challenge those who possess it and are responsible for its affairs and try to wrestle it from them." Except if you see, as the Messenger of Allāh *(sallallāhu alayhi wassallam)* stated, *"clear explicit (buwāhan) kufr"*, which is apparent, explicit and uncovered in which there is no difference or doubt regarding it. Importantly, this is not to be decided upon by the common people or by the riff-raff and rabble, rather this is decided upon by the people of knowledge who are firmly grounded in knowledge as they are the people who understand the state of affairs and estimate it with a just estimation. *"Until you see clear (buwāhan) kufr, for which you have with you evidence from Allāh."* Shaykhul-Islām ibn Taymiyyah *(rahimahullāh)* appended to this *hadeeth* in his book *Minhāj us-Sunnah* saying: **'This issue is a clear obligation from the Prophet (sallallāhu alayhi wassallam) even if the ruler takes from the people unjustly and gives precedence to himself over the people and falls in oppression. But this hadeeth prohibits us from challenging the rulers and trying to wrestle rulership from them.'** Meaning: even if they are oppressors, it is incumbent to obey them and if they take anything without right it still is not permissible to revolt against them. He continued saying: **'This is a prohibition of revolting against them as they are the people who wield the reins of leadership, Allāh** has commanded us to obey them and they have the power and they utilise it to fulfil what they do.'[201] Imām al-Kirmānī, who has an explanation of Saheeh Bukhārī before al-Hāfidh ibn Hajar and in fact Ibn Hajar benefited from his explanation, stated: **'This hadeeth indicates that a ruler should not be toppled due to his fisq (sin) because in doing so would lead to tribulation, blood-shed, dissension and enmity and the harms of this is much worse than the harm of him remaining in his position of leadership.'**

There is another *hadeeth* which certifies the same meaning of preventing revolting against the leaders, rulers and those in charge of the responsibilities. It is the *hadeeth* which is also in *Saheeh Muslim* from Umm Salamah *(radi Allāhu 'anha)* wherein she said: "The Messenger of Allāh *(sallallāhu alayhi wassallam)* said: *"Rulers will gain authority over you. You will know, recognise and accept that which is righteous and you will reject that which is evil.*[202] *So whoever hates that has freed himself and whoever gives advice has saved himself, but the problem is with the ones who are satisfied and go along with that (evil)."* They (the companions) said: "Should we not fight them?" He *(sallallāhu alayhi wassallam)* said *"No! As long they pray"* and in another *hadeeth "No! As long as they establish the prayer"* meaning: as long as they permit you to pray and the prayer is the greatest practical symbol of Islām so as long as the prayer is established and permitted then this is the greatest sign of Islām after the two testimonies of faith. Ibn Taymiyyah stated in *Minhaj us-Sunnah*, vol.3, p.392:

فقد فمى رسول الله صلى الله عليه وسلم عن قتالهم مع إخباره أفهم يأتون
أمورا منكرة فدل على أنه لا يجوز الإنكار عليهم بالسيف كما يراه من
يقاتل ولاة الأمر من الخوارج والزيدية والمعتزلة وطائفة من الفقهاء وغيرهم

The Messenger of Allāh forbade the Muslims from fighting against the rulers along with informing the Muslims that they will see some sins (from the leaders). This indicates that it is impermissible to revolt against the rulers by means of the sword (i.e. with weapons) as the Khawārij, Zaydiyyah, Mu'tazilah and a group of fuqahā view as permissible.

Shaykh ul-Islām Ibn Taymiyyah stated about the revolt of Husayn *(radi Allāhu 'anhu)* in *Minhāj us-Sunnah*, vol.4, p.530:

ولهذا لما أراد الحسين رضي الله عنه أن يخرج إلى أهل العراق لما كاتبوه كتبا
كثيرة أشار عليه أفاضل أهل العلم والدين كابن عمر وابن عباس وأبي بكر
بن عبد الرحمن بن الحارث بن هشام أن لا يخرج وغلب على ظنهم أنه يقتل
حتى إن بعضهم قال أستودعك الله من قتيل وقال بعضهم لولا الشفاعة
لأمسكتك ومصلحة المسلمين والله ورسوله إنما يأمر بالصلاح لا بالفساد
لكن الرأي يصيب تارة ويخطيء أخرى

فتبين أن الأمر على ما قاله أولئك ولم يكن في الخروج لا مصلحة دين ولا
مصلحة دنيا بل تمكن أولئك الظلمة الطغاة من سبط رسول الله صلى الله
عليه وسلم حتى قتلوه مظلوما شهيدا وكان في خروجه وقتله من الفساد ما
لم يكن حصل لو قعد في بلده فإن ما قصده من تحصيل الخير ودفع الشر لم
يحصل منه شيء بل زاد الشر بخروجه وقتله ونقصالخير بذلك وصار ذلك
سببا لشر عظيم وكان قتل الحسين مما أوجب الفتن كما كان قتل عثمان مما
أوجب الفتن

وهذا كله مما يبين أن ما أمر به النبي صلى الله عليه وسلم من الصبر على
جور الأئمة وترك قتالهم والخروج عليهم هو أصلح الأمور للعباد في المعاش
والمعاد وأن من خالف ذلك متعمدا أو مخطئا لم يحصل بفعله صلاح بل فساد
ولهذا أثنى النبي صلى الله عليه وسلم على الحسن بقوله إن ابني هذا سيد
وسيصلح الله به بين فئتين عظيمتين من المسلمين ولم يثن على أحد لا بقتال
في فتنة ولا بخروج على الأئمة ولا نزع يد من طاعة ولا مفارقة للجماعة

For this reason, when Husayn (radi Allāhu 'anhu) wanted to go out to
the people of 'Irāq after they had written many letters to him. The
notables of the people of knowledge and deen such as Ibn 'Umar, Ibn

159

'Abbās and Abū Bakr ibn 'AbdirRahmān ibn il-Hārith ibn il-Hishām advised him not to go as they thought that he would be killed.[203] To the extent that some of them said "may you place your trust in Allāh from being killed."[204] It would emerge that the affair was as they had said and there was not in his (Husayn's) insurrection any benefit for the deen and no benefit for the dunya[205], rather those oppressors and transgressors were established in the earth, and they seized him until he was killed unjustly and was martyred. And in his insurrection and murder was immense corruption which would not have occurred had he remained in his country. He only intended to establish good and ward off evil, yet he did not achieve anything.[206] Rather, evil increased in his revolt and due to his death and good was diminished with that and that (his revolt and subsequent death which had occurred as a result of the action) became a reason for great evil. As the killing of Husayn caused tribulation just as the killing of 'Uthmān caused tribulation. So all of this makes clear that what the Prophet (sallallāhu 'alayhi wassallam) instructed regarding patience with the oppression of leaders and avoiding fighting them or trying to revolt against them is the most rectifying affair of the servants (of Allāh) in the dunya and the Hereafter and whoever opposed this intentionally[207] or mistakenly,[208] no rectification was realised with his action rather corruption. For this reason, the Prophet (sallallāhu 'alayhi wassallam) praised his grandson Hasan[209] by saying "my son here is a Sayyid and through him Allāh will resolve a matter between two great groups of the Muslims."[210] The Prophet (sallallāhu 'alayhi wassallam) did not praise anyone for fighting during a tribulation, for revolting against the leaders, for withdrawing obedience from the ruler or for splitting off from the jamā'ah (the congregation of Muslims).

Ibn Abi'l-'Izz al-Hanafī in *Sharh ut-Tahāwiyyah*, p.370 mentions:

وأما لزوم طاعتهم وإن جاروا؛ لأنه يترتب على الخروج من طاعتهم من المفاسد أضعاف ما يحصل من جورهم بل في الصبر على جورهم تكفير السيئات ومضاعفة الأجور، فإن الله تعالى ما سلطهم علينا إلا لفساد

أعمالنا و الجزاء من جنس العمل. فعلينا الاجتهاد في الاستغفار والتوبة

وإصلاح العمل. فإذا أراد الرعية أن يتخلصوا من ظلم الأمير الظالم

فليتركوا الظلم...

Adhering to obedience to them (i.e. the leaders), even if they oppress, because revolting against them will result in greater corruptions than their oppression. Rather, to be patient with their transgression absolves one from evil actions and multiplies the rewards. Allāh has only placed such leaders over us due to our corrupt actions so the results are from the actions being done, so it is for us to strive in seeking forgiveness from Allāh and to repent and rectify our actions...**So if the people want to be free from the oppression of the oppressive leader they have to leave off oppression themselves.**

Imām Ahmad mentions in his *Usūl us-Sunnah* that revolt against a Muslim leader is not to be made. He states under point 53:

And whoever revolts against a leader from among the leaders of the Muslims, after the people have agreed upon him and united themselves behind him, after they had affirmed the khilāfah for him, in whatever way this khilāfah may have been, by their pleasure and acceptance or by (his) force and domination (over them) - then this revolter has disobeyed the Muslims, and has contradicted the narrations of the Messenger of Allāh (sallallāhu 'alayhi wassallam). And if the one who revolted against the ruler died he would have died the death of ignorance.

Then point 54:

And the killing of the one in power is neither lawful nor permissible for anyone amongst the people to revolt against him. Whoever does that is an innovator, (and is) upon other than the Sunnah and the (correct) path.[211]

Therefore, the claim of Omar Bakrī in his treatise on *Ahl us-Sunnah* in ftn.123 on page 111 of his ebook on the 'aqeedah of Ahl us-Sunnah wa'l-Jama'ah that **"Imām Ahmed rose against and publicly championed people against the state..."** is false. Ibn Taymiyyah stated:

The *Sahābah (ridwānullāhi 'alayhim)* used to pray behind those whose sin they knew about as 'Abdullāh ibn Mas'ood and others prayed behind al-Waleed bin 'Uqbah bin Abī Mu'eet and he used to drink alcohol. He prayed *Subh* with four *Rakāts* and 'Uthmān ibn 'Affān whipped him for that. 'Abdullāh bin 'Umar and other Sahābah used to pray behind al-Hajjāj bin Yūsuf and the Companions and Successors used to pray behind Ibn Abī 'Ubayd who was accused of *Ilhād* and calling to misguidance.[212]

'Aqeedah on Dealing with the Rulers from Imām Abū Ibrāheem Ismā'īl bin Yahyā al-Muzanī (d. 264 AH)[213]:

He was the author of *Sharh us-Sunnah* and was an Imām of the Muslims, the *'Ulama* testified to his knowledge, virtue, *zuhd* (asceticism) and *wara'* (abstemiousness). He is Abū Ibrāheem Ismā'īl bin Yahyā al-Muzanī, the companion of ash-Shāfi'ī, he died in 264 AH. This Imām lived through the reign of eleven different *khulafā'* from the Abbasid Empire:

- Hāroon ar-Rasheed (d.193 AH/809 CE)
- Muhammad al-Ameen (d.198 AH/814 CE)
- Al-Ma'moon (d.218 AH/833 CE)[214]
- Al-Mu'tasim (d. 227 AH/842 CE)[215]
- Al-Wāthiq (d. 232 AH/847 CE)[216]
- Al-Mutawakkil (d. 247AH/861 CE)[217]
- Al-Muntasir (d. 248 AH/862 CE)
- Al-Musta'een (d. 252 AH/866 CE)
- Al-Mu'tazz (d. 255 AH/869 CE)
- Al-Muhtadī (d. 256 AH/870 CE)
- Al-Mu'tamid (d. 279 AH/892 CE)

This Imām lived in Egypt among a large portion of *Huffadh, Muhadditheen, Fuqahā, Qurā', Zuhhād* and others. Such as the likes of:

- The 'Ālim of Egypt Abū Muhammad 'Abdullāh Ibn Wahb al-Fihrī (d. 197 AH);
- Imām Abū 'Abdillāh ibn Idrees ash-Shāfi'ī (d. 204 AH), who was with al-Muzanī a lot and affected him greatly.
- The *Muhaddith* of Egypt Sa'eed Abū Maryam al-Hāfidh (d. 224 AH)

- The Shaykh of Egypt Harmalah bin Yahyā at-Tujaybī al-Hāfidh al-Faqeeh, the compiler of *al-Mukhtasar* and *al-Mabsūt*, he died in 223 AH
- Hāfidh ul-Misr Ahmad ibn Sālih al-Misrī, one of the notable who died in 248 AH

Outside of Egypt during the time of al-Muzanī were:

- Sufyān bin 'Uyaynah, the Shaykh of the Hijāz who died in 197 AH
- The *Hāfidh* of the era Abū Dāwūd Sulaymān bin Dāwūd at-Tayālsī (d.204 AH)
- Shaykh ul-Ummah Ahmad bin Hanbal (d. 241 AH)
- Shaykh ul-Islām, the *Hāfidh* of the era Muhammad bin Ismā'īl al-Bukhārī (d. 256 AH)
- The *Hāfidh* of Khurasān,[218] Muslim bin al-Hajjāj al-Qushayrī (d. 261 AH)

There were other scholars who were contemporaries of al-Muzanī and during this time there were great academic achievements wherein the scholars authored precious compilations, classifications and books and the treatise of al-Muzanī was influential during that time. He was born in the year when al-Layth bin Sa'd died 175 AH[219] and it is apparent that his family had a love for knowledge and its people and they had a righteous and academic upbringing. The scholars of al-Muzanī's sister mentioned that she used to attend the gatherings of knowledge given by Imām ash-Shāfi'ī and ar-Rāfi'ī used to transmitted narrations from her in his Book of *Zakat*.[220] Ibn us-Subkī mentioned her, as did al-Isnawī in *at-Tabaqāt*.[221] His biographers do not go in depth in mentioning his teachers rather they restrict them to the following:

1. Muhammad ibn Idrees ash-Shāfi'ī[222]
2. 'Ali bin Ma'bad bin Shaddād al-Basrī[223]
3. Nu'aym bin Hammād[224]
4. Asbagh bin Nāfi'[225]

Ibn Yūnus stated in his *Tāreekh*: [226]

The companion of ash-Shāfi'ī; he was of great worship and virtue, trustworthy in *hadeeth*, the dexterous scholars did not differ over him, he was one of those who was abstinent in the *Dunya* and was from the best of Allāh's creation, his qualities are many.[227]

Abū Ishāq ash-Shīrāzī stated: "He was an ascetic scholar, a debater, a proof, immersed in the detailed meanings."[228] 'Amru bin 'Uthmān al-Makkī said:

I have not seen anyone with abundant worship from those who I have met from the people of Makkah than him. I have not met anyone from the people of Shām and Alexandria and its surrounding areas and fortified areas with such efforts as al-Muzanī. I have not seen anyone as constant in worship than him and I have not seen anyone who has exalted knowledge and its people than al-Muzanī, he was the most intense on himself in *wara'* which he bequeathed to the people. He used to say: "I am merely from the characteristics of ash-Shāfi'ī *(rahimahullāh).*[229]

Abū Sa'eed bin as-Sakkarī stated: "When I saw al-Muzanī I realised that I had not seen anyone who worships Allāh more than him or understands the details of *fiqh* more than him."[230] Al-'Abbādī said: "He was an ascetic and abstemious scholar, he had nice statements when debating..."[231] Ibn 'AbdulBarr stated:

He was a scholar and *Faqeeh*, a well known reference point, he had great abilities in debating and had understanding of the different aspects of speech and argumentation. He had good speech and was the foremost from the *madhdhab* of Shāfi'ī and his statements, memorising its principles with precision. He has many books in the Shāfi'ī *madhdhab* that no one else ever equalled. The people tired after him, he was the most knowledgeable from the companions of Shāfi'ī in debating, he had detailed knowledge and his books and abridgements circulated throughout the different regions of the earth, east and west. He was pious, abstinent, religious and patient with little and got by with simple-living.[232]

Ibn ul-Jawzī said:

The companion of Shāfi'ī *(rahimahullāh);* he was a deft *Faqeeh*, trustworthy in *hadeeth* and was of abundant worship and virtue. He was from the best and gracious of Allāh's creation and adhered to the fortified frontline areas (*Ribāt*).[233]

Ibn Khallikān said: "The Imām of the Shāfi'īs and the most knowledgeable of them of his way (i.e. the way of Shāfi'ī), his *fatāwā* and whatever had been transmitted from him."[234] Adh-Dhahabī said: "The Imām, 'Allāmah, Faqeeh of the religion, the knowledgeable Zāhid."[235] As-Subkī stated: "The great Imām, the supporter of the madhdhab, a mountain of knowledge, the decisive debater, the Zāhid, the abstemious, the one detached from the Dunya."[236] Al-Isnawī (772 AH/1371 CE) stated: "He was a pious Imām and Zāhid, detached from the dunya, exalted among the companions of Shāfi'ī."[237] In Sharh us-Sunnah, points 14 and 15 states:

14 - Obedience to the People in Authority in that which pleases Allāh and staying away from whatever angers Allāh.[238]

15 – Withholding from making takfeer of the people of the Qiblah (i.e. Muslims) and being free from whatever they do as long as they do not innovate any misguidance. Whoever of them innovates any misguidance is outside the fold of the people of the Qiblah and has departed from the deen. So one gains nearness to Allāh by freeing oneself from him, abandoning him, hating him and staying away from what he has innovated.

'Aqeedah on Dealing with the Rulers from Imām Abū 'Uthmān as-Sābūnī (d. 449 AH):

He stated in 'Aqeedat us-Salaf wa As-hāb ul-Hadeeth:

The People of Hadeeth view the establishment of Jumu'ah, the two 'Eids and other prayers behind a Muslim Imām, righteous or sinful, as long as he is not a disbeliever who is outside the fold of the religion.[239] They (the People of Hadeeth) make du'ā for the Muslim rulers for success and righteousness,[240] and they[241] do not view (that it is permissible to make) revolt against them (the Muslim rulers) even if they see from them deviation from justice towards injustice, oppression, transgression and its likes.[242]

'Aqeedah on Dealing with the Rulers from Imām Ahmad bin Hanbal (d.241 AH):

Imām Ahmad mentions in his Usūl us-Sunnah that revolt against a Muslim leader is not to be made. He states under point 53:

And whoever revolts against a leader from among the leaders of the Muslims, after the people had agreed upon him and united

165

themselves behind him, after they had affirmed the khilāfah for him, in whatever way this khilāfah may have been, by their pleasure and acceptance or by (his) force and domination (over them), then this revolter has disobeyed the Muslims, and has contradicted the narrations of the Messenger of Allāh (sallallāhu alayhi wassallam). And if the one who revolted against the ruler died he would have died the death of ignorance.

Then point 54:

And the killing of the one in power is not lawful, and nor is it permissible for anyone amongst the people to revolt against him. Whoever does that is an innovator, (and is) upon other than the Sunnah and the (correct) path.[243]

Therefore, the claim of Omar Bakrī in his treatise on *Ahl us-Sunnah* in ftn.123 on page 111 of his ebook which has been linked to previously that "Imām Ahmed rose against and publically championed people against the state..." is false.

THE EDUCATION AND CREDENTIALS OF
OMAR BAKRĪ MUHAMMAD FUSTUQ

Bakrī claimed in his book *Essential Fiqh* (London: Islāmic Book Company, 1996) that he graduated from numerous universities, the most of important of which being *Umm ul-Qura'* in Makkah, the *Islāmic University of Madeenah* and *al-Azhar* in Egypt, along with the *College of Sharee'ah* in Damascus!!?[244]

In a document authored by Omar Bakrī entitled *The Islāmic Verdict on Jihad and the Method to Establish the Khilafah* a different biography of where Bakrī studied is given wherein his *tadlees*[245] can again be viewed, the pdf can be read here: http://osolihin.files.wordpress.com/2007/03/jihad-and-methodology.pdf

Firstly, on page 4 of the book in the 'about the author' section it claims that Bakrī is:

Sheikh Omar bin Bakrī bin Muhammad is from Aleppo, Syria. He was born in 1958 and brought up amongst an orthodox and rich Muslim family. He is married and father of six children. Sheikh Omar started to study Islām, the sciences of Qur'ān, The Sciences of Hadith, the sciences of Usul Al-Fiqh, the Islāmic law and systems from his childhood until today. He is quality {sic} of knowledge is a Mujjtahid Murajjih Juristic Scholars {sic} able to outweigh {sic} between the four Islāmic Schools of thought: Hanafi, Maliki, Shafi'ie and Hanbali. {sic} Sheikh Omar adopted the Aqeedah of Ahl Al-Sunnah Wa Al-Jama'ah and adopted the Shafi'ie Mazzhab {sic}. Currently He {sic} is preparing his Ph.D. in the Science of Islāmic Inheriting or I'lm {sic} Al-Mirāth. He received his BA in Shari'ah and the foundations of The Islāmic Jurisprudence from the Shari'ah University in Damascus-Syria. He received his MA in the Islāmic Jurisprudence (Al-Fiqh) of The four Schools of thought from the University of Al-Imam Al-U'zaie-Beirut. He accompanied and studied with many qualified scholars of Islām like sheikh Abdullah Al-Zamalkāni, Sheikh Osama Al-Khani, Sheikh Awadh Al-Dimashqui and Sheikh Al-Zuheili from Damascus. He joined many Islāmic movements like Al-Ikhwān, Al-Tali'ah, Ebād Al- Rahman, Hizb ut-Tahrir and Al-Muhajiroun. He is the founder of Hizb ut- Tahrir UK branch and the founder of Al-Muhajiroun world-wide. Sheikh Omar written {sic} and published many articles and leaflets, he participated in a number of conferences on various aspects of topics {sic}. In addition to being a speaker and Khateeb in many Mosques, he also has audio and visual productions, including commentary on the Qur'ān. He is currently the judge of the Shari'ah court for the UK, The {sic} Secretary General of The {sic} Islāmic World League, The {sic} principal lecturer of the London school of Shari'ah and The {sic} Leader of Al-Muhajiroun.[246]

So it claims that Bakrī was preparing a Ph.D in the science of "Islāmic Inheriting" {sic}, yet in which university was he doing this and what is the name of the institution? If it was deemed as important to mention that he is doing a Ph.D then mention where this is being conducted aswell! Secondly, it is insinuated that Bakrī studied with "Shaykh Zuhaylī" and he intends by this Wahbah az-Zuhaylī, the famous scholar of *fiqh* in Syria. As a result of this, in the late 90s some Muslim students from London travelled to Syria and had the opportunity to meet Wahbah az-Zuhaylī. They asked him if Omar Bakrī really is a bona fide student of his and Wahbah az-Zuhaylī denied even knowing anyone called Omar Bakrī! When Bakrī was approached over this by the Muslim students from London, Bakrī's response was: "No, no, not that Zuhaylī, another Zuhaylī!" Clear *tadlees*! Thirdly, it is stated that Bakrī was a: **"speaker and khateeb in many mosques"** (!!?) this is false, as Bakrī was not allowed to conduct his frolics in most of the *Masājid* in London, let alone being a speaker in "many mosques"! So we see here that Bakrī is merely trying to build up his CV and résumé and make it more colourful than it actually is!

What is also immediately noticeable within the above mentioned biography is that any mention of having been at *Umm ul-Qura University* in Makkah, the *Islāmic University of Madeenah* and *al-Azhar University* in Cairo has all also miraculously disappeared from his CV!? This was due to 'AbdurRahmān Dimishqiyya exposing the deceptions of Bakrī in the late 1990s.[247] Yet we still come across gross inconsistencies and blatant *tadlees* within his biography, indeed, we further come across the following about Bakrī:

He is currently the judge of the Shari'ah court for the UK, The {sic} Secretary General of The {sic} Islāmic World League, The {sic} principal lecturer of the London school of Shari'ah and The {sic} Leader of Al-Muhajiroun.

La hawla wa la quwwata ila billāh! Since when was Bakrī a "judge" meaning that he is a fully qualified Qādī! And where is this **"Shari'ah Court for the UK"**? As for him being the **"Secretary-General of the Islāmic World League"** then this again is another example of *tadlees*. For what they are doing here is playing with the name of the other organisation which is well known as being the *Muslim World League*. So Bakrī is trying to assert that he is the Secretary General of the *MWL* and as for being the **"Secretary-General of the Islāmic World League"** then where is this organisation? Why the trickery and *tadlees*? The same is again observed when it states that he was the **"principal lecturer of the London school of Shari'ah"**, but where is this school? What's the address and what do they study? Who are the teachers and what is the curriculum? It seems to only exist within their fanciful imaginations that are coupled with delusions of grandeur. All to bolster their CVs and credentials in the eyes of Muslim youth this is the extent that some will go to.

On Yawm ul-Ahad 2nd Shawwāl 1428 AH/Sunday October 14th 2007 CE, the disgraced fraud appealed on *al-Jazeera* (Arabic) TV for the British government to grant him his civil rights and to give him his British residency status back!!!?[248] However, he neither pronounced his request on any English channels nor on his own English language website! So at this former website here for example 'Obmonline.net', which was set up by *al-Muhajiroun*, there was no mention whatsoever of his recent appeal for his beloved British residency status to be returned and this again demonstrates the deceptive tactics of Bakrī. So while he appeals for his beloved British residency status to be given back to him on Arabic TV he continues promoting *takfeer, ghuloo* and ignorant concepts of jihad amongst English speaking youth who do not understand Arabic!

The only article that we found had picked up on the story was an article by Muhammad ash-Shāfi'ī in *ash-Sharq al-Awsat* (London), dated with the same date mentioned above when he was on *al-Jazeera*, the story can be read in Arabic here[249]:

The article says:

بكري: أطالب بريطانيا بمحاكمتي أو السماح لي بالعودة لرؤية أولادي

الإسلامي السوري لــ «الشرق الأوسط»: أنا محاصر من كل مكان

وتركت عملي.. وقوات الأمن اللبنانية رحلت 14 إسلاميا من تلامذتي

Bakrī: "I request Britain to judge me or allow me to return to see my children."
The Syrian Islāmist says to ash-Sharq al-Awsat: "I am isolated from everywhere and I have left my work...the Lebanese Security forces have deported 14 Islāmists who are my students".

لندن: محمد الشافعي

قال الإسلامي السوري عمر بكري فستق المقيم في بيروت انه يخضع

لضغوط امنية تحاصره من كل مكان، مما اضطره الى مغادرة وقف اقرأ

الذي كان يعمل فيه، وكذلك مدينة طرابلس الى العاصمة بيروت».

وأوضح بكري الممنوع من دخول بريطانيا، انه يعيش حالة مأساوية في

شقته بعيدا عن عائلته التي تعيش في بريطانيا. وقال انه سيزور السفارة

البريطانية غدا وسيتحدى قرار منع عودته الى العاصمة البريطانية من

اجل حضور العملية الجراحية الخطرة التي ستجريها ابنته راية الإسلام.

وقال بكري في اتصال هاتفي أجرته معه «الشرق الأوسط»:«إما أن

توجه لي السلطات البريطانية تهمة مثبتة وتطالب بسجني، أو أن تعلن

السلطات البريطانية بأنني لست مطلوبا لها ولا متهما بأية جريمة، وفي

هذه الحالة يمكنني العودة الى أهلي». وقال ان الضغوط الأمنية التي

170

يتعرض لها في لبنان اضطرته الى مغادرة مكتبة الوقف الإسلامي في طرابلس بشمال لبنان، وحرمته من الحصول على أي تأشيرة للسفر».

وتساءل: «لماذا كل هذه الضغوط على أمثالي هذا ظلم كبير، والظلم ظلمات». واوضح: «أريد أن يسمع العالم وأن يعرف بأنني لم أرتكب جريمة قط في حياتي، وما هذا أعامل معاملة المطلوبين الفارين، وأحرم من حقوقي المدنية، إما أن تثبت بريطانيا للعالم بأنني قد ارتكبت جريمتي على أراضيها وتطالب بسجني، أو أن تعلن بأني بريء من التهم الإعلامية التي توجه لي من قبل بعض وسائل الإعلام الغربية». وقال: «كل ما أريده الآن، استرجاع حقي في إمكانية زيارة أولادي ولو لأيام معدودة».

London: Muhammad ash-Shafi'ī

The Syrian Islāmist, Omar Bakrī Fustuq resident in Beirut, said that he is subject to pressure from security surrounded everywhere, which forced him to leave the Iqra Foundation where he had worked, as well as the city of Tripoli to the capital Beirut. Bakrī was barred from entering Britain and said that he is in a tragic situation in his apartment away from his family living in Britain. He said that he will visit the British embassy tomorrow and challenge the decision to prohibit his return to the British capital to be there for the operation on his daughter (named) Rā'yat ul-Islām. Bakrī said in a telephone interview with «ash-Sharq al-Awsat»: «Either the British authorities charge me with that which is affirmed and imprison me, or the British authorities declare that I am neither wanted nor accused of any crime, in which case I can return to my family». He said that the security in Lebanon compelled him to leave the Islāmic endowment office in Tripoli in northern Lebanon, and deprive him of access to any kind of visa for travel». He asked: «Why is there all this pressure on the likes of me, all of this great injustice and darkness».[250] He explained: «I want to let the world know that I have never committed a crime ever in my life, so what is this "wanted fugitive" treatment? I am being deprived of my civil rights. So either Britain proves to the world that I have committed crimes on its territory and seeks my imprisonment, or they declare that I am innocent of the charges directed me by some Western media». He said: «All I want now is the possibility of recovery of my right to visit my children even for a few days».

وضمن الضغوط التي تعرض لها بكري على حد قوله لـ«الشرق الأوسط» تم ترحيل أكثر من 14 شابا من تلامذته على دفعات بعد ان جاءوا لزيارته في لبنان، كان آخرهم أصولي مقيم في احد فنادق العاصمة بيروت، ذهب لزيارته الأسبوع الماضي، فأبلغ مدير الفندق اجهزة الأمن. وأشار الى أن الأمن العام اللبناني طلب منه نصح جميع الإخوة البريطانيين بعدم محاولة زيارته في لبنان إن كانت عندهم نية لقائه ولو للحظة. ورغم معرفة بكري بأن أمر عودته الى بريطانيا معقد بحسب محاميه، الا انه طالب بريطانيا بمحاكمته وتوجيه أي اتهام له أو السماح له بالعودة لرؤية أولاده الستة، وأحفاده الخمسة وزوجته، وحضور الجراحة العاجلة لابنته راية الإسلام.

Among the pressures brought to bear on him which Bakrī objected to he told «ash-Sharq al-Awsat» were that more than 14 young people from his students have been deported after they came to visit him in Lebanon. One of them was a fundamentalist residing in a hotel in the capital, Beirut. He went to visit him (i.e. Bakrī) last week, and the hotel manager activated the Security devices and informed the Lebanese Public Security who then asked Bakrī to advise all British brothers not to attempt to visit Lebanon if they have the intention of meeting him even for a moment. Although Bakrī knows that his return to Britain depends on his lawyer, he still called for

172

Britain to either try him and charge him of any accusation or allow him to return to see his six children, five grandchildren and his wife, and attend urgent surgery for his daughter Rā'yatul-Islām.

In order to demonstrate some of his frolics within the Arabic media, which are not featured on the site run by his British blind followers, we will relay another article here which we have abridged:

FIRST – 'Omar Bakrī Denounces "Sheikh Google"', 18ᵀᴴ AUGUST 2007 by Mohammad Al-Shafey in ash-Sharq al-Awsat[251]:

London, Asharq Al-Awsat- Today, Omar Bakrī rejects being labeled as the Islāmic fundamentalist who once led the al Muhajiroun and al Ghurabā movements and prefers the title 'expert in Islāmist movements.' In this interview with Asharq Al Awsat, the notorious preacher, who left Britain after 20 years for Lebanon following the 7/7 attacks, calls for establishing peace and the sparing of Muslim blood in what seems to be far removed from the heated slogans of the fundamentalists that he once led and the calls for establishing "Londonistan".

Q: Many observers believe that the tone of your speeches that are delivered in Lebanon has changed and is more composed in comparison to the speeches delivered in London. What is the reason for this change?

A: My Islāmic speeches have not changed. My interviews are characterized by politeness and composure coupled with firmness. At demonstrations and rallies, my speeches are strong. Of course, for every occasion there is a suitable address. A sincere observer of my live speeches in London would have noticed that they were characterized by originality, clarity, and firm ideas, and that they were completely different from what some western media conveyed after subjecting them to censorship, editing, and distortion that changed the meaning and distorted the ideas. This has been and remains the case in the British newspapers, as I have been exposed to a widespread media smear campaign in Britain. However, I think that the real cause [behind the perceived change] lies in the fact that some Lebanese media organizations have dealt with me in a transparent way that was not the case with many western media organizations, or even with the famous Arab television satellite channels, except in the interviews that were broadcast by the BBC channels and Sky News. There is no doubt that my appearance in the Lebanese media, with such transparency, has been my golden opportunity to respond to the media charges that the western media and newspapers accuse me of. It has been a great opportunity for me to speak to the people live on the air - **as an expert on Islāmist movements** - without being defamed, and to be able to focus on the ideas rather than spending time rejecting lies. This used to happen in Britain a lot during interviews and people would think that the accusations were true if I did not refute them to save time in the interview. Lebanese newspapers and magazines have conducted many interviews with me without distorting or changing what I say. I was surprised by the sincerity of the Lebanese press, at least with me personally; despite the political and sectarian inclinations of these newspapers and magazines.

Q: Are you still committed to your previous statements, such as, 'The flag of Islām will fly over Buckingham Palace and the White House,' and 'the magnificent 19' [a reference to the 9/11 hijackers]?

A: I still am committed to, and proud of all the statements that I have made that have been published without being distorted. These statements are issued purely for the sake of God, and I ask God to accept them, and to add them to our share of good deeds on the Day of Judgment. These statements include inviting Queen Elizabeth, all MPs, and the British people in general to convert to Islām, my comment that the Islāmic preaching will continue until the flag of Islām will fly over British Parliament, the royal palace, the White House, and the entire world, and my statement that a Muslim who plays an active role in preaching and who lives among non-Muslims in Britain or any other country is not allowed attack other people.

As for the statements that have been attributed falsely to me or to my followers, such as the statement that Islām permits the destruction of children's schools, the killing of women, children, and the innocent, that Britain is a toilet for the Muslims, and other trivia and falsehoods; such comments have been spread to harm us.

Q: How would you describe yourself today? Are you a Salafist? Do you still believe in the concept of the Caliphate?

A: There are bound to be disputes among people because God Almighty says in Surah Hud, Verse 118/119: 'If thy Lord had so willed, He could have made mankind one people: but they will not cease to dispute. Except those on whom thy Lord hath bestowed His Mercy: and for this did He create them.' We have been told about these disputes and divisions in the Hadith by Al Tabarani who said that the Prophet (PBUH) said, 'My nation is divided into 73 groups, all of which will be in Hellfire except one.' They asked him, 'What is this group?' He said, 'They are those who are upon like what I am upon today and my Companions.' Praise be to God who guided and honored me by joining the groups of the Prophet (PBUH).

I am a Salafist Muslim in my creed and in my ways because God Almighty has praised and recommended this as He addressed His Messenger (PBUH) and his companions, may God be satisfied with them, in Surah Al Baqarah, Verse 137: 'So if they believe as ye believe, they are indeed on the right path; but if they turn back, it is they who are in schism; but God will suffice thee as against them.' Therefore, whoever agrees with the creed and way of our righteous predecessors, i.e. God's Messenger, his companions, and his household, is guided by God, and whoever disagrees with them is one of the people of the schism.[252] There is no doubt that collective work towards preaching God's word and for the establishment of the Islāmic caliphate is a Shariah duty to which I am committed in the same way that I am committed to prayers and to fasting. This has to be done in a clear way according to Shariah, which is calling for God through wisdom, good advice, and the promotion of virtue and prevention of vice.

Q: It is argued that Islāmic preachers were the safety valve in Britain before the 7/7 attacks in London. The proof of this is that most of your students were arrested after you left Britain. What is your comment in this respect?

A: I believe that the British people were safer when the Islāmic preachers in Britain were free because these preachers were able to control and rationalize the anger of the Muslim youths in Britain,[253]

175

caused by the government's hostile policies towards issues related to Islām, and the double-standards in dealing with the Palestinian issue in favor of the Israeli enemy...

Q: What are you doing in Tripoli?

A: My duty as a Muslim is to preach God's religion according to the way of the righteous predecessors. As for the reality of the Lebanese arena, I live among a complex secular society where many parties are classified on sectarian and ideological bases; there is harmony among the various spectra of the Lebanese fabric despite the push-and-pull, convulsions, and sectarian tensions. As for my work in the Lebanese arena, currently, I am the director general of the Iqra Library for general reading and academic research, and a member of the Shariah committee of Iqra Islāmic Trust in Tripoli in the Abu-Samra district. I address the Lebanese society via a number of television channels as an (Islāmic) expert in the affairs of Islāmic groups; this is in addition to writing for some Lebanese newspapers, taking part in educational activity by teaching the foundations of jurisprudence to Iqra's academic group, and other weekly activities such as Quran interpretation, Friday sermons, and other open dialogues aimed at enriching Islāmic thinking in Lebanon...

Q: How do you survive away from your family, loved ones, and friends in Britain? How do you communicate with your children?

A: The critical security situation in Lebanon, the sectarian tension, the repeated Israeli aggressions, the political tension represented by the sit-ins by the opposition forces in the center of Beirut, the resulting consequences such as the events of Al-Jadida Road and the accompanying closure of streets and burning of cars, the closure of the airport, and the Nahr al-Bared crisis and the accompanying bloody confrontations in Tripoli where I moved to after the painful events of Beirut; all these unstable conditions have forced me to live away from my wife, my children, and my grandchildren. I live away from my family that still lives in the same house in Britain where I had lived for more than 20 years before I left Britain out of my own free will. The declaration by the British government to withdraw my residence on its territories did not surprise me, because during my entire legal residence in Britain I did not accept British citizenship

176

for reasons related to Shariah. **However, I was surprised by the decision to deprive me of the right to visit my wife, my six children, and my five grandchildren, as they all have British citizenship.** The fact is that I live alone in an apartment in Tripoli; in addition to the pains of longing to see the family and loved ones, I bear the burden of cooking, cleaning, washing, ironing, and so on. However, praise be to God, I communicate with my wife, my children, and my friends in Britain through the Internet and the telephone.

Q: Is there a certain mosque in which you preach in Tripoli?

A: I am not an employee of the official Lebanese Dar al-Fatwa. I am not an official of any mosque in Lebanon. I am an independent Islāmic preacher, and I deliver most of my lessons in the halls of the academic library. I deliver my Wednesday weekly lecture in Al-Qasimiya mosque in old Tripoli. Some Imams invite me to deliver the Friday sermon as a guest in a number of mosques in Tripoli and other Lebanese cities, and I preach in the English language in some Lebanese universities and colleges.

Q: Do you feel that there is a difference today between the Muslims amongst whom you live in northern Lebanon, and the Muslims to whom you used to preach in Europe?

A: The truth is that the Islāmic commitment and Islāmic preaching that I saw in Britain was stronger among the Muslims in Britain than in Lebanon. They were more cohesive, better established, and more sincere. This is because in Britain there are no nationalistic or ethnic inclinations between the Arab Muslims and non-Arabs. Moreover, the Muslims in Britain are economically independent and financially successful, a fact that allows them to be free from slavery and those who try to exploit their conditions. The call to non-Muslims to convert to Islām in Britain is stronger, better known, and more successful than it is in Lebanon, because of the absence of political sectarianism. Therefore, the rate of conversions to Islām in Britain is over 18 people a day.[254] The Christian sect in Lebanon is politicized; also the Muslims practice political activity on religious sectarian basis. These sectarian obstacles make inviting non-Muslims to convert to Islām difficult and infrequent.

Q: What is your opinion on the statement that has been attributed to you that the recent foiled attacks were the result of young people influenced by "Sheikh Google," and "Sheikh Yahoo"?

A: I still believe that Muslim youths in Britain today lack Islāmic authority and that Britain is short of Islāmic preachers who the youth can trust, and who are capable of guiding the youth so that they do not fall prey to those who believe that there are no pledges or security between the Muslims living in Britain and the non-Muslims. Because of the failure of the so-called "moderate Islāmic organizations" that are loyal to the British government to attract Muslim youths, some of these youngsters resort to "Sheikh Google" or "Sheikh Yahoo," i.e. the Internet in search for fatwas, which were the reasons behind the failed attacks in London. They might find a religious ruling on the internet that is suitable for the situation in Afghanistan and Iraq, but unsuitable for the situation in Britain.

Q: **Are you thinking of returning to Britain after the change in government and following Britain's call for handing over the Guantanamo detainees who were living in Britain?**

A: **If the British authorities grant me a visa for a visit, I will visit my family and my loved ones in Britain, but the issue of returning to live in Britain would mean that I would sue the Home Office in the British courts. This is not allowed by Shariah and is not going to happen, because I am not going to resort to the man-made British courts to restore my permanent residence, which was withdrawn by the British Home Office.[255] Bear in mind that I have not been charged with any crime in Britain or in any other country. Some British human rights and judicial organizations might call for allowing me to return in order to bring the family together again and because so far I have not been charged with any crime in Britain.**

He is also known for making very extreme statements via the media yet was never ever apprehended by the British government for his incitement and agitation. So for example, on 19 April 2004 in an interview with a Portuguese magazine called *Publica*, Bakri stated:

"**It's inevitable. Because several attacks are being prepared by several groups...one very well organized group in London calling** itself 'al Qaeda Europe' appears has a great appeal for young Muslims. I know that they are ready to launch a big operation."[256]

In January 2005 CE Bakri, via live internet broadcasts urged British Muslims to join al-Qā'ida and that the British government had violated the 'covenant of security' due to their anti-terror legislation. He asserted that the UK had become Dār ul-Harb. Nafeez Mosaddeq Ahmed highlights:

> Bakri's statements clearly suggest that he had advance warning of the plans to conduct a domestic terrorist attack in London by a British-based group, al-Qaeda in Europe. This, in turn, suggests that he was in a position to be directly acquainted with the relevant terrorist planning; and by implication that being so acquainted, he must have had sufficient contact with the planners and/or their terrorist associates.[257]

Ahmed also mentions:

> Further firm evidence of a direct connection between the bombers and al-Muhajiroun came in the form of a confession made by al-Qaeda suspect Muhammad Junaid Babar, detained in New York for attending an al-Qaeda terror summit in Pakistan. Babar admitted to US authorities that he knew the chief London bomber, Mohammed Siddique Khan. Babar was a member of the Queens branch of al-Muhajiroun. Reportedly part of a terrorist network in Pakistan, Babar was also connected with the March 2004 plot uncovered by the police. After pleading guilty in June 2004, he turned informant for the security services.[258]

Bakri boasted in a 2002 interview: **"The British government knows who we are. MI5 has interrogated us many times. I think now we have something called public immunity."**[259]

Also, al-Muhajiroun published 'fatāwā' from Bakri inciting acts of violence and terrorism against governments including: a death threat against the Pakistani military leader Musharraf, after making takfeer on him after 9/11 on BBC news in September 2001; a call to kill Boris Yeltsin and even a call to assassinate Tony Blair in 2004 branding him a "legitimate target"!!? Yet no action was taken against al-Muhajiroun. Bakri had already made takfeer of the Tālibān regime in August 2001 CE in a letter that Bakri wrote to Mullah 'Umar wherein he branded Afghānistān as 'Dār ul-Kufr' under the Tālibān and not an abode of Islām!? See: 'Ash-Sharq al-Awsat'

179

newspaper; no. 2 August 2001 CE. Bakri also boasted that his brother had joined *al-Qā'ida* and had received a one year course in weapons and evasive vehicle manoeuvring in Texas and Scotland!!? With regards to all of this Nafeez Ahmed states:

These selected citations are only a small representative sample of hundreds of inflammatory anecdotes, documents and speeches made by Bakri and other leading members of al-Muhajiroun. Inciting people to violence breaks existing UK law and under normal circumstances would lead to arrests, charges, prosecution, and in appropriate cases, deportation. After the London bombings, the government called for new legal powers to tackle terrorism. But this only highlights the question of why the government failed to use the powers it already had?[260]

Nafeez Ahmed then superbly notes:

The security and intelligence services knew that al-Muhajiroun was recruiting aggressively and successfully in the UK. They knew that individuals radicalized by the group had fought and died in Afghanistan. By consistently refusing to arrest and charge members of al-Muhajiroun for their post-9/11 terrorist training and recruitment programme, which by their own proud admission allowed British Muslims to be trained in al-Qaeda camps in Afghanistan in preparation for future terrorist operations on UK soil, British authorities left intact the networks that radicalized Siddique Khan and his companions. We have had no explanation for this apparent lapse...[261]

180

CONCLUSION

This study demonstrates conclusively and emphatically the futility of masquerading behind a noble title, because a name without substance is nothing but a label, as the saying goes:

»لسان الحال أبين من لسان المقال«

A person's condition is clearer than verbal expression
(i.e.: 'Actions speak louder than words')

As the 'Ulama of Usūl say:

»العبرة بالحقائق والمعاني لا بالألفاظ والمباني«

"What are important are the realities and the meanings (that are applied), not terms and structures"
(so if there is a contradiction between a term and the reality of what is being manifest then the reality and what it means is what is of importance, despite the use of a mere term)

And as the 'Ulama of Usūl also emphasise:

»ادعاء المُسميات لا يُلزم ثبوت الصفات«

"Claiming names does not necessitate affirmation of the characteristics (of those names)"

Without a doubt, these observations also indicate that the cult of Omar Bakrī Muhammad Fustuq, al-Muhajiroun, is a partisan political phenomenon which adapts itself to the fluctuations of the geo-political order to convince unsuspecting Muslim youth that they are the flag-bearers of the truth. This study further shows that the cult of Omar Bakrī is an erratic ever-changing *hizb*, which in its endeavour to wield control over the Muslim youth, will adopt a whole range of guises, gowns and images in order to infiltrate the generality of the Muslim populace.

What has this *hizb* achieved by hijacking the noble title of our forefathers, except confusion and chaos? However this group is not alone in its abuse of the term "Salafi" for it is also a common feature of various misguided groups to cloak their deviant ways under the innocent title of 'Salafiyyah'. So is it enough in our times to rely purely on a hollow slogan to find the correct group which is at harmony with the truth, echoed for eternity in the words of the Prophet Muhammad (*sallallāhu 'alayhi wassallam*) when he said: *"There will not cease to be a group from my Ummah*

181

clearly apparent on the truth"²⁶²? Or is it an obligation for every Muslim to look behind the mere rhetoric of a name or title to recognize its reality?

One must stress here that we are not in any way attempting to undermine the noble tradition of affiliating oneself to *Sharee'ah* advocated titles as an introductory method to initially clarify the real flag bearers. We only voice our criticism here when the titles are unfortunately hijacked and abused by those who have no right to adorn such titles. We live in strange times, where people of the Sunnah are few but their titles are many, whereas those who preceded us in righteousness and piety, were many and their titles were few. These words encapsulate the predicament which plagues us in modern times. However, by the grace of Allāh the Muslim scholars have been on hand to correct this misuse and abuse of the title 'Salafi'. Shaykh 'AbdulMālik ar-Ramadānī al-Jazā'irī, an Algerian *Salafi* scholar, stated about the Algerian *takfiri* group known as the *'Salafi Group for Da'wah and Combat'*:

How can, with all of this, making permissible the blood of the police and killing them, be clean (i.e. permitted)? Then they live on stolen monies which have been ransacked from people by force! They destroy the souls of the Muslim soldiers...As a result, we do not however absolve ourselves from 'Salafiyyah' as it is the truth, yet we absolve ourselves for Allāh from the 'Salafist Group for Dawah and Combat' and from all those who grasp weapons today in our country against the system or the people. I say this so that the creation know that the ascription of those revolutionary groups (i.e. the GSPC) to Salafiyyah is a distortion of Salafiyyah, just as how ascribing deviant Muslims to Islām is also a distortion of Islām, blocking the true path of Allāh and causing people to flee from the victorious ones (firqat un-Nājiyah). However, Salafiyyah is Salafiyyah, just as Islām is Islām, even though it is distorted by the deviants.²⁶³

Shaykh 'AbdusSalām bin Sālim bin Rajā' as-Sihaymī (Associate Professor at the *Department of Fiqh* of the *Sharee'ah College*, the *Islāmic University of Madeenah*) stated in his book *Kun Salafiyyan 'ala'l-Jādah* [Be a Serious Salafi], after mentioning the words of King 'Abdul'Azeez Āli-Sa'ud:

These are precious words which exemplify the correct meaning of Salafiyyah which in itself exemplifies the correct Islām. In these days Islām generally and the Kingdom of Saudi Arabia²⁶⁴ along with the da'wah Salafiyyah specifically[265], have bore the brunt of falsehood, oppression, confusion and things which are not the reality. This has been due to some politicians, Western writers who hate Islām and those who promote the Zionists and their views agreeing with their oppression and falsehood and have thus been influenced by them in certain countries. This is even though the Da'wah Salafiyyah is the furthest from takfeer (to brand a Muslim as an disbeliever), tabdī' (to brand a Muslim as an innovator) and tafseeq (to brand a Muslim as a sinner) without evidence, it is also the furthest from extremism and fanaticism. Yet this blessed da'wah has been associated with things which are not from it and it has been ascribed to things which are not from its manhaj which all distorts it beauty and reality. One of the most glaring factors for this is: the existence of contemporary partisan Islāmic groups affected by the Khawārij ideology and their well-known leaders agreed with a few things from the Salafi manhaj in some matters.[266] Indeed, some of them even spoke in the name of Salafiyyah when the reality is that they were not from it and this confused many people and the reality was hidden from them as they thought that these groups were Salafi or "Wahhabi" as some of them named it. What is really strange is that some of these partisan Islāmic groups named themselves "Salafi Jihadis", yet how can they be Salafi when they oppose its 'aqeedah and manhaj?! The reality however is in the application and meanings not in mere terms and names and as a result it is a must to bring attention to this confusion and misguidance which is present in the Islāmic world today.[267]

No matter how much effort these wolves invest in fashioning their sheep's clothing, their fraudulent ways and lies will always be discovered, eventually.[268]

1 Saheeh al-Bukhārī vol. 1, no. 100 and Saheeh Muslim.

2 Ibn Mājah, Saheeh.

3 The cult followers of Omar Bakrī Muhammad change their names in order to hide, this is a common aspect of their recent manifestation.

4 His ignorance can also be seen here with the following lectures: http://uk.youtube.com/watch?v=LSSV1ca-lkM Yet be aware that many of his videos have been removed particularly after the Online version of this book was made available.

5 Refer to: http://www.dailymail.co.uk/news/article-1054909/Have-babies-Muslims-UK-hate-fanatic-says-warning-comes-9-11-UK.html

6 He can be seen here attempting to justify his stances, his lack of knowledge is noticeable: http://www.youtube.com/watch?v=R2JbsTMj0Yw&feature=related

7 For more on this issue refer to: Shaykh 'AbdusSalām bin Sālim Rajā' as-Sihaymī (Associate Professor in the Department of Fiqh, College of Sharee'ah, Islamic University of Madeenah), *Kun Salafian 'alā'l-Jādah!* [Be a Serious Salafi!] (Cairo: Dār ul-Manhaj, 1426 AH/2005). With introductions by Shaykh 'Ali bin Muhammad bin Nāsir al-Faqīhī and Shaykh 'Ubayd bin 'Abdullāh al-Jābirī.

8 Al-Bukhārī, *as-Saheeh, hadeeth* no.5752; Muslim, *as-Saheeh, hadeeth* no. 60

9 Al-Bukhārī, *as-Saheeh, hadeeth* no.48; Muslim, *as-Saheeh, hadeeth* no. 64

10 Reported by at-Tabarānī from the *hadeeth* of Hishām bin 'Urwah – *hadeeth* graded *Saheeh* by al-Albānī as in *Saheeh al-Jāmi' as-Sagheer* (1269).

11 Also refer to page 29 of the following with regards to the Ottoman Caliph Sulayman (1520 -1566 CE) and his adaptation of law, which earned him the name "Kanūnī": http://www.arts.ualberta.ca/~amcdouga/Hist323/lecturespdf/suleiman_the_magnificent.pdf

12 Carter V. Findlay, *The Turks in World History* (New York: Oxford University Press, 2005), pp.116-117.

13 Stanford J. Shaw and Ezel Kural Shaw, *History of the Ottoman Empire and Modern History: Volume 1, Empire of the Gazis/The Rise and Decline of the Ottoman Empire 1280-1808* (Cambridge, London and New York: Cambridge University Press, 1976), p.134.

[14] Juan Ricardo Cole, *Colonialism and Revolution in the Middle-East: Social and Cultural Origins of Egypt's 'Urabi Movement* (Cairo; American University in Cairo Press, 1999), p.40

[15] Antony Black, *The History of Islamic Political Thought: From the Prophet to the Present* (New York: Routeledge, 2001), p.210

[16] Sami Zubaida, *Law and Power in the Islamic World* (New York: I.B. Tauris, 2005), pp.107-108.

[17] Ibid., p.112

[18] Ibid.

[19] *Majmū' al-Fatāwā*, vol.2, p.267

[20] *Majmū' al-Fatāwā*, vol.11, p.507

[21] *ad-Durarus-Sunniyyah fil-Ajwibatun-Najdiyyah* vol.7,p.239

[22] Refer to the book by Professor Sulaiman Bin Abdurrahman al-Huqail (Professor of Education at Imām Muhammad bin Saud University, Riyadh), *Muhammad Bin Abdulwahhâb – His Life and the Essence of his Call* (Riyadh: Ministry of Islamic Affairs, Endowments, Dawah and Guidance, KSA, First Edition, 1421 AH/2001 CE), with an introduction by Sheikh Saleh Bin Abdulaziz Al-Sheikh.

[23] Abdul'Azeez ibn Muhammad Āl 'AbdulLateef, *Da'āwa al-Munāwi'een li Da'wat al-Shaykh Muhammad ibn 'Abd al-Wahāb* (Riyadh: Dār ul-Watan, 1412 AH), p. 233

[24] *Majmoo'at Mu'allafāt al-Shaykh*, vol.5, p.11

[25] *Majmoo'ah Mu'allafāt al-Shaykh*, vol.1, p.394; quoted in *Da'āwa al-Munāwi'een*, pp.233-234

[26] *'Aqeedat al-Shaykh Muhammad ibn 'Abd al-Wahhāb wa atharuha fi'l-'Ālam al-Islami* (unpublished), vol.1, p.27

[27] 'Abdullāh ibn Sālih al-'Uthaymeen, *ash-Shaykh Muhammad ibn 'Abd al-Wahhāb Hayātuhu wa Fikruhu* (Riyadh: Dār ul-'Ulūm, 1412 AH) p.11; quoted in *Da'āwa al-Munāwi'een*, pp.234-235.

[28] Refer to these maps of the Ottoman Empire which clearly show that the Ottomans did not have authority in Najd, just as the Ottomans had no authority in West Africa, hence Shaykh Uthmān Dan Fodio establishing his own Caliphate well known as the Sokoto Caliphate. Likewise, the Ottomans had no authority in Morocco which was ruled by the *'Alawi* dynasty and India was ruled by the Mughal Empire. Also the Ottomans had no authority in Sudan. See:

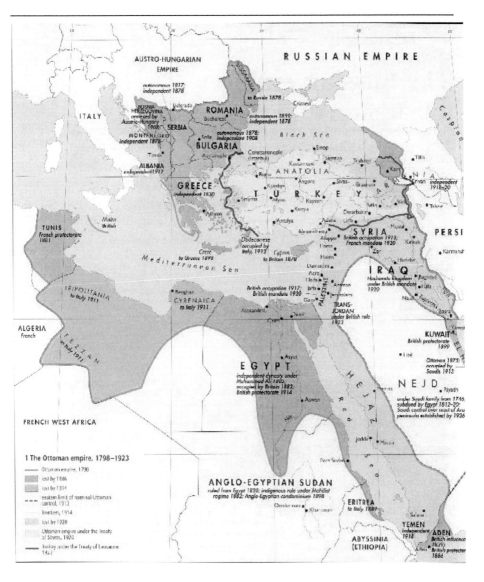

Ottoman Empire, 1798-1923: See:
http://ww1.huntingdon.edu/jlewis/syl/IRcomp/MapsOttoman.htm

186

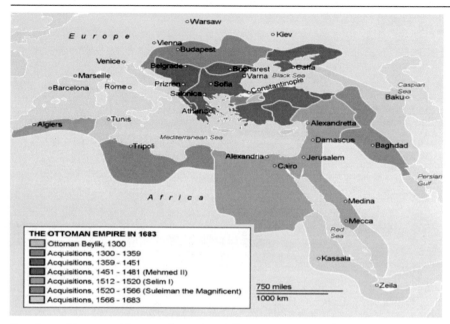

See: http://www.mideastweb.org/Middle-East-Encyclopedia/ottoman.htm

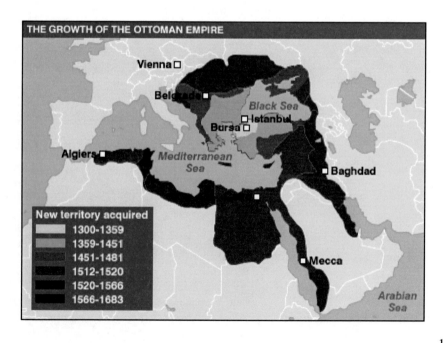

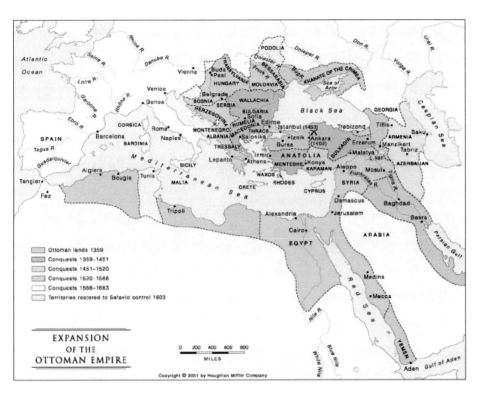

☐	Ottoman lands 1359
☐	Conquests 1359–1451
☐	Conquests 1451–1520
☐	Conquests 1520–1566
☐	Conquests 1566–1683
☐	Territories restored to Safavid control 1603

EXPANSION
OF THE
OTTOMAN EMPIRE

0   200   400   600   800
MILES

Copyright © 2001 by Houghton Mifflin Company

188

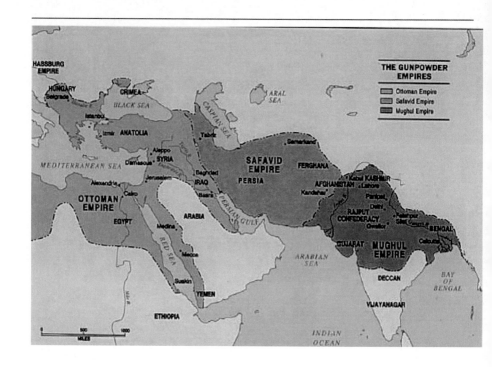

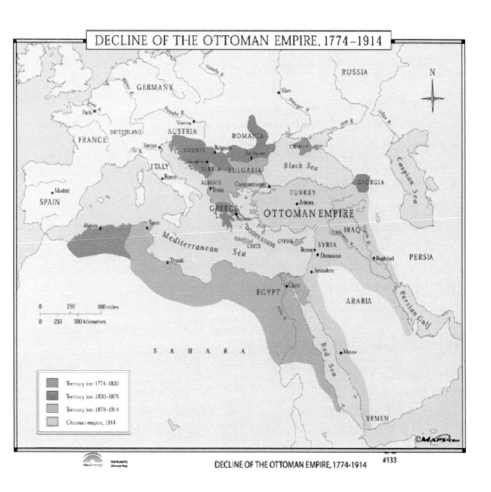

DECLINE OF THE OTTOMAN EMPIRE, 1774-1914

#133

190

See: http://worldmapsonline.com/UnivHist/30335_6.gif

[29] Conversation recorded on tape; quoted in *Da'āwa al-Munāwi'een*, p. 237

[30] *Majallat al-Mujtama'*, issue no. 510

[31] *Al-Mujtama'*, issue no. 504; quoted in *Da'āwa al-Munāwi'een*, p. 238-239

[32] *Al-Shaykh Muhammad ibn 'Abd al-Wahhāb fī Mar'āt al-Sharq wa'l-Gharb*, p. 240

[33] Ibid. p. 64

[34] Adapted from *Majmū' Mu'allafāt is'-Shaykh*, vol.5, p.189

[35] Ibid. vol.5, p.25

[36] Ibid. vol.5, pp.11-12, 62

[37] Ibid. vol.3, p.11

[38] Ibid. vol.5, p.100

[39] Muhammad Basheer ash-Sahaswani, *Siyānat ul-Insān min Wasawis id-Dahlān* (Riyadh: Najd Press, 1396 AH), p.485

[40] Taken from *ad-Durar-us-Saniyyah* [The Personal Letters of ash-Shaykh Muhammad bin 'Abdil-Wahhāb *(rahimahullāh)*] letter no.19 page 57 and originally translated by Aboo 'Imraan al-Mekseekee.

[41] Selim Deringil *(Boğaziçi University*, History Department), *The Turks and Europe: Uninvited Guests of Sharers of a Common Destiny?* Paper presented to the *Center for European Studies*, 24 February 2005.

[42] For more on this refer to:

   ✓ Khaled Fahmy, *All the Pasha's Men: Mehmed Ali, his Army and the Making of Modern Egypt* (Cambridge, UK: Cambridge University Press, 1997), pp.274-278.

   ✓ Andrew James McGregor, *A Military History of Modern Egypt: From the Ottoman Conquest to the Ramadan War* (Westport, Conneticut. : Praeger Security International, *2006*), pp.116-120

[43] Suraiya N. Faroqhi (ed.), *The Cambridge History of Turkey: Vol.3, The Later Ottoman Empire 1603-1839* (Cambridge, UK: Cambridge University Press, 2006), p.106.

[44] The roots of this war go back to 1851 when the French forced the Ottomans to make them the "sovereign Christian authority" of the Holy Land which the Russians rejected due to two treaties which were previously made with the Ottomans in 1757

and 1774. The Ottomans thus reversed their decisions and made the Russians the official sovereign Christian authority of the Holy Land and then the French responded with a show of military force in the Black Sea forcing Sultān 'AbdulMajeed I to change his mind. The newest treaty, between France and the Ottomans, confirmed France and the Catholic Church as the supreme Christian organization in the Holy Land, supreme control over the various Christian holy places, and gave the keys to the *Church of the Nativity*, previously in the hands of the Greek Orthodox Church to the Catholic Church. Angry at this, the Russian Tsar sent the 4th and 5th army corps to be deployed and mobilised along the Danube River.

The Russians tried to negotiate another treaty wherein they would regain authority over the Christian communities within the Ottoman Empire and the British Prime Minster of the day, Aberdeen, encouraged the Ottomans to reject this, which led to war. Benjamin Disraeli blamed Aberdeen and Stratford (who negotiated with the Ottomans on behalf of the British) for causing the war and this led to Aberdeen's resignation from office. After a diplomatic process the Sultan proceeded to war, his armies attacked the Russian army near the Danube and the Russian Tsar Nicholas responded by dispatching warships, which destroyed a squadron of Ottoman frigates in northern Turkey at the Battle of Sinop on 30 November 1853. The destruction of the Turkish fleet and heavy Ottoman casualties alarmed both Great Britain and France, which stepped forth in defence of the Ottoman Empire. In 1853, after Russia ignored an Anglo-French ultimatum to withdraw from the Danubian Principalities, Great Britain and France thus declared war.

[45] Who conquered much of the Algerian coast and announced they were rulers of it, as the British were 'masters' of India.

[46] For more on this refer to James J. Reid, *Crisis of the Ottoman Empire: Prelude to Collapse 1839-1878* (Stuttgart: Franz Steiner Verlag, 2000), pp.175-235. Also refer to Virginia H. Aksan, *Ottoman Wars 1700-1870: An Empire Besieged* (Harlow, England : *Longman*/Pearson, *2007*).

[47] Lubna A. Alam, *Keeping the State Out: The Separation of Law and State in Classical Islamic Law* (Reviewing Rudolph Peters, Crime and Punishment in Islamic Law: Theory and Practice from the Sixteenth to the Twenty-First Century), *105 Michigan Law Review*, pp. 1255-1264 (April 2007):
http://www.michiganlawreview.org/archive/105/6/alam.pdf

48 Ihsan Yilmaz, *Muslim Law, Politics and Society in Modern Nation States – Dynamic Legal Pluralisms in England, Turkey and Pakistan* (Aldershot, UK: Ashgate, 2005), p.90.

49 http://www.anayasa.gen.tr/1876constitution.htm

50 Ihsan Yilmaz, *op.cit.*, p.92.

51 'AbdurRahmān ad-Dimishqiyyah produced evidence for this in his book *Hizb ut-Tahreer* (Istanbool, Turkey: Maktabah al-Ghurabā', 1417 AH/1997 CE), pp.63-66.

52 Bukhārī and Muslim

53 Al-'Allāmah al-Muhaqqiq Abū Ishāq Ibrāheem bin Mūsā bin Muhammad al- ash-Shātibī (d.790 AH/1388 CE), Abū 'Ubaydah Mashhūr bin Hasan Āl Salmān (ed.), *al-I'tisām* (Ammān: ad-Dār ul-Athariyyah, 1428 AH/2007 CE), vol.2, p.167.

54 Ibid., p.128

55 Recorded by al-Fasawī in *al-Ma'rifah wa't-Tāreekh*, vol.1, p.670; al-Khateeb al-Baghdādee, *al-Faqeeh wa'l-Mutafaqqih*, vol.2, p.324, no.1039; Ibn 'AbdulBarr, *Jāmi' Bayān ul-'Ilm*, vol.2, p.1225, no.2410; Ibn us-Salāh, *Adab al-Muftī wa'l-Mustaftī*, p.85; Ibn ul-Jawzī, Mashhūr Hasan (ed.), *Ta'dheem ul-Futyā*, p.112, no.46; at-Tartūshī, *al-Hawādith wa'l-Bida'*, p.70; Abū Shāmah, Mashhūr Hasan (ed.), *al-Bā'ith*, p.179.

56 Meaning a Mujtahid who gives rulings based on the Usūl of the Imām of his madhhab and confines his rulings to the main source books of his madhhab.

57 Imām ash-Shāfi'ī, Ahmad Shākir (ed.), *ar-Risālah* (Beirut: al-Maktabah al-'Ilmiyyah, n.d.).

58 Imām ash-Shāfi'ī, 'Ali Sinān (ed.), *Ibtāl ul-Istihsān* (Beirut: Dār ul-Qalam, 1406 AH).

59 Ibn 'AbdulBarr, *Jāmi' Bayān ul-'Ilm wa Fadlihi* (Beirut: Dār ul-Kutub al-'Ilmiyyah, n.d.)

60 Ibn Qudāmah, *Rawdat un-Nādhir wa Jannat ul-Manādhir* (Beirut: Dār ul-Kutub al-'Ilmiyyah, n.d.).

61 Shaykh ul-Islām Ibn Taymiyyah, 'AbduRahmān bin Qāsim and his sons (eds.), *Majmoo' al-Fatāwā* (Makkah: Maktabat un-Nahdah al-Hadeethah, 1404 AH).

62 Ibn ul-Qayyim, TaHa 'Abdur-Ra'oof Sa'd (ed.), *I'lām ul-Muwaqqi'een 'an Rabb il-'Ālameen* (Beirut: Dār ul-Jaleel, 1973 CE).

[63] Ibn un-Najjār al-Fatūhī, Dr Muhammad az-Zuhaylī and Nazeeh Hammād (eds.), *Sharh ul-Kawkab il-Muneer* (Makkah: Markaz al-Bahth al-'Ilmi, Umm ul-Qura University, n.d.)

[64] Shaykh Muhammad al-Ameen ash-Shinqītī, *Mudhakkirat Usūl ul-Fiqh* (Madeenah: al-Maktabah as-Salafiyyah, n.d.).

[65] Refer to Muhammad bin Husayn bin Hasan al-Jīzānī, *Ma'ālim Usūl ul-Fiqh 'inda Ahl is-Sunnah wa'l-Jama'ah* [Signposts of Islamic Legal Principles According to Ahl us-Sunnah wa'l-Jama'ah] (Dammām, KSA: Dār Ibn ul-Jawzī, 1428 AH/2007 CE), pp. 472-478, 509-517.

[66] These classical definitions have been emphasised by Imām Muhammad bin 'AbdulWahhāb in *Kitāb ut-Tawheed* and *Thalathat ul-Usūl,* also refer to Shaykh Muhammad bin 'AbdulWahhāb al-Wassābī's *Qawl ul-Mufeed fī adillat it-Tawheed,* these works have been translated into English. For a book written in English and specifically directed to Western readers refer to *Fundamentals of Tawheed* by Dr Abu Ameenah Bilal Philips.

[67] http://video.google.com/videoplay?docid=-2560493866437684563

[68] Zakariyyā bin Ghulām Qādir al-Pākistānī, *Tawdeeh Usūl il-Fiqh 'ala Manhaj Ahl il-Hadeeth* [Elucidation of Legal Theory in Accordance with the Methodology of the People of Hadeeth] (Dammām, KSA: Dār Ibn ul-Jawzī), p.29.

[69] For the blog of Adam Deen refer to: http://adamdeen.blogspot.com/

[70] Reported by Abū Dāwūd, at-Tirmidhī and Ibn Mājah and it is Saheeh.

[71] *Majmoo' al-Fatāwā Ibn Bāz*, vol.8, p.182

[72] Shaykh, Dr Sālih bin Fawzān al-Fawzān, Muhammad bin Fadh al-Husayn (ed.), *al-Ijabāt al-Muhimmah fi'l-Mashākil al-Mumilah* (Riyadh: Matābi' al-Humaydī, 1425 AH/2004 CE, 2nd Edn.), p.156.

[73] Ibid., p.155.

[74] The ISBN numbers for this book, which is still available via *Amazon* for example, are: **ISBN 10: 1899534008** and **ISBN 13: 978-1899534005**. The book is also available via the website *Lawbooks Online,* conduct search here: http://www.lawbooks-online.com/index.asp?search=bic&bic=LXP&offset=80

[75] 'AbdurRahmān ibn Muhammad Sa'eed Dimashqiyyah, *Hizb ut-Tahreer* (Istanbool, Turkey: Maktabah al-Ghurabā', 1417 AH/1997 CE), pp.63-66.

194

[76] For more on what the Salafi scholars have said on the issue of *al-Hākimiyyah*, refer to what has been translated on this issue by Aboo Iyyād Amjad Rafeeq of *Salafi Publications*   here:
http://www.salafipublications.com/sps/sp.cfm?secID=MNJ&subsecID=MNJ07&loadpage=displaysubsection.cfm

[77] *Liqā`ul Maftooh* (no. 150) 20th *Shawwāl* 1417 AH

[78] http://www.youtube.com/watch?v=zOv5X18SD9w

[79] Part 3 of the Press TV interview on *youtube*.

[80] Al-Bukhārī, *as-Saheeh*, hadeeth no.5752; Muslim, *as-Saheeh*, hadeeth no. 60

[81] Allāh says,

$$﴿إِنَّ اللَّهَ لاَ يُغَيِّرُ مَا بِقَوْمٍ حَتَّى يُغَيِّرُواْ مَا بِأَنفُسِهِمْ﴾$$

"Indeed, Allāh will not change the condition of a people until they change what is in themselves."

{ar-Ra'd (13): 11}

Allāh also says,

$$﴿وَكَذَلِكَ نُوَلِّى بَعْضَ الظَّـلِمِينَ بَعْضاً بِمَا كَانُواْ يَكْسِبُونَ﴾$$

"And thus will We make some of the wrongdoers allies of others for what they used to earn."

{al-An'ām (6): 129}

And Allāh says,

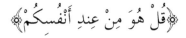

"Say it is from yourselves (i.e. due to your sin)..."

{Āli-'Imrān (3): 165}

And Allāh says,

195

﴾ظَهَرَ الْفَسَادُ فِي الْبَرِّ وَالْبَحْرِ بِمَا كَسَبَتْ أَيْدِي النَّاسِ لِيُذِيقَهُم

بَعْضَ الَّذِي عَمِلُوا لَعَلَّهُمْ يَرْجِعُونَ﴾

"Corruption has appeared throughout the land and sea by [reason of]
what the hands of people have earned so He may let them taste part of
[the consequence of] what they have done that perhaps they will return
[to righteousness]."

{Room (30): 41}

82 Refer to the pronouncements and statements of Omar Bakrī's followers, such as
what can be read here: http://www.islam4uk.com/aqeedah/tawheed
Their websites however change nearly every four months, but their views are still the
same regardless.

83 http://video.google.com/videoplay?docid=-2560493866437684563

84 http://video.google.com/videoplay?docid=-2560493866437684563

85 See Shaykh 'Ali bin Yahyā al-Hadādī's research on this matter in his book *al-Ghulū
wa Madhāhirahu fī Hayāt il-Mu'āsirah* (Cairo: Dār ul-Manhāj, 1426 AH/2005 CE),
pp. 42-55. The book also has introductions from Shaykh Wasīullāh bin Muhammad
'Abbās *(hafidhahullāh)* and Shaykh Ahmad bin Yahyā an-Najmī *(rahimahullāh)*.
here: http://www.salafimanhaj.com/pdf/SalafiManhaj_Extremism.pdf

86 http://adamdeen.blogspot.com/

87 Scholars of the past allowed the use of non-Muslim, *kuffār* and *mushrik* forces to
be drafted upon for Muslims, if there is a benefit in that for the Muslims. Such as:

- Imām ash-Shāfi'ī *(rahimahullāh)*
- Imām Ahmad ibn Hanbal *(rahimahullāh)*
- Imām Abu'l-Qāsim al-Khirqī *(rahimahullāh)*
- Imām Abu'l-Hasan as-Sindī *(rahimahullāh)*
- Imām Bin Bāz *(rahimahullāh)*
- Imām Ibn 'Uthaymeen *(rahimahullāh)*

Therefore, this shows that the issue of drafting *kuffār* forces is something which was
said by scholars in the past and the scholars who also ruled this in the present era

were thus preceded in their rulings. Ibn Qudāmah al-Maqdisī *(rahimahullāh)* stated in *al-Mugnī* (vol.13, p.98):

> **Help is not to be sought from a mushrik, this is what Ibn al-Mundhir, al-Jūzjānī and a group of the people of knowledge said. There is present from Ahmad what indicates the permissibility of gaining assistance from them (i.e. mushrikeen) and the statements of al-Khirqī also indicate that, if there is a need and this is the school of thought of Shāfiʾī.**

Imām an-Nawawī stated in his explanation, vol.11-12, p.403, under *hadeeth* no.4677:

> **His saying (sallallāhu alayhi wassallam): "Go back, for I do not seek help from a mushrik; and it is mentioned in another hadeeth that the Prophet (sallallāhu alayhi wassallam) sought help from Safwān bin Umayyah before his Islām, as a result some scholars give the first hadeeth precedence over the second one. Imām Shāfiʾī and others said: If the disbeliver has good opinion of the Muslims and the need has come to utilize him, of not then he is disliked. So these two hadeeths are taken in light of two circumstances.**

Shaykh Abu'l-Hasan as-Sindī stated in his explanation of the *hadeeth "I do not gain assistance from a mushrik"*, from the *Sunan Ibn Mājah* (vol.3, p.376, under *hadeeth* no.2832):

> **It shows that gaining assistance from a mushrik is harām without a need. But if there is a need then it can be done as an exception and this is not opposed.**

From: Bandar bin Nāʾif bin Sanahāt al-'Utaybī, *Wa Jādilhum Bilatī Hiya Ahsan, Munāqishatun 'Ilmiyyatun Hādiyyatun li-19 Mas'alatin Muta'alaqatin bi-Hukkām il-Muslimeen* (Riyadh: Maktabah 'AbdulMusawwir bin Muhammad bin 'Abdullāh, 1427AH/2006 CE, Fourth Edition), pp.38-42.

[88] For example, in the following video Omar Bakrī Muhammad Fustuq praises Abu Mus'ab az-Zarqawi, makes *takfeer* of King Fahd and refers to the so-called "magnificent 19": http://www.youtube.com/watch?v=guQhWjm6do8

[89] Refer to pp.28-48 of: http://www.salafimanhaj.com/pdf/SalafiManhaj_TakfeerAndBombing.pdf

Ibn Taymiyyah also said:

197

This was the result of patience and consciousness of Allāh which Allāh instructed (the Muslims to have) at the very beginning of Islām and during that time the jizya was not taken from any of the Jewish community, or other non-Muslim communities, who were living in Madeenah. Those verses applicable to every Muslim in a state of weakness who is not able to aid Allāh and His messenger with his hand or via his tongue (i.e. by speaking), but could help by using what he was able to by his heart and the likes. The verses about subduing those non-Muslims who have contracts with Muslims are applicable to every strong believer who is able to help the deen of Allāh and His Messenger with his hand and tongue (i.e. via speaking). It is with these verses that the Muslims were applying during the last epoch of the Messenger of Allāh (sallallāhu alayhi wassallam) and during the epoch of his rightly guided caliphs. And thus it will be until the Day of Judgement as there will never cease to be a group from this ummah who are well established on the truth who help Allāh and His Messenger with complete help. So whoever from the believers is weak in the earth or is weak in the time in which he is living in, must apply those verses of the Qur'ān which mention patience and forgiveness against those who are seeking to harm Allāh and His Messenger from those who were given the scriptures prior and also from the polytheists. As for those people who are in a state of strength then they are to apply the verses regarding fighting the leaders of kufr who slander the deen. They are also to apply the Qur'anic verses regarding fighting those who were given the scriptures prior until they pay the jizya and are subjugated.

Refer to Ibn Taymiyyah, *as-Sārim al-Maslool*, vol.2, p.413.

90 http://www.youtube.com/watch?v=Eq7IkMKLAok

91 http://www.youtube.com/watch?v=guQhWjm6do8

92 http://uk.youtube.com/watch?v=uv704B93EZU&NR=1

93 Reported by Muslim in *Kitāb ul-Jihād* and within other chapters, vol.3, p.1356, *hadeeth* no.1731.

94 The addition of **"…and those in monasteries (or other places of worship)"** is from the *Musnad* of Imām Ahmad, vol.5, p.352.

95 Reported by Mālik in the *Muwatta'*, *Kitāb ul-Jihād* in the chapter of the prohibition of killing women and children during warfare, vol.2, p.447, the *hadeeth* is on the authority of Yahyā bin Sa'eed from Abū Bakr as-Siddeeq that he said the *hadeeth*. 'AbdurRazzāq also reported the *hadeeth* in *Kitāb ul-Jihād* in the chapter of *'destroying the trees within the land of the enemy'*, vol.5, p.199, *hadeeth* no.9375 on the authority of Ibn Jurayj who said: Yahyā bin Sa'eed said that Abū Bakr said, then he mentioned the *hadeeth*. The *isnad* is *munqati'* (disconnected) but the *'Ulama* have utilised it and referred to it as the meaning is correct and in agreement with other authentic *marfoo'* narrations.

Shaykh Mashhūr Hasan Āl Salmān mentions that Yahyā bin Sa'eed did not hear directly from Abū Bakr as-Siddeeq. The *hadeeth* was also reported by Sa'eed bin Mansūr, *Sunan*, (no. 2284); al-Bayhaqee, *Sunan*, vol.9, p.86; al-Balādhurī, *Ansāb ul-Ashrāf*, pp.108-09 via another route of transmission from Abū Bakr, see *al-Majālisah*, p.1535 and *Jāmi' il-Usool*, vol.2, p.599.

In the *Sunan* of Abū Dawūd, *Kitāb ul-Jihād* is the following *hadeeth* on the authority of Anas bin Mālik *(radi Allāhu 'anhu)*: The Prophet *(sallallāhu'alayhi wassallam)* said: *"Go in Allāh's name, trusting in Allāh, and adhering to the religion of Allāh's Messenger. Do not kill a decrepit old man, or a young infant, or a child, or a woman; do not be dishonest about booty, but collect your spoils, do right and act well, for Allāh loves those who do well."*

Imām Ibn ul-Munāsif (563-620 AH) states in his *magnum opus* on jihad entitled *Kitāb ul-Injād fi Abwāb il-Jihād*:

As for the insane person then there should be no difference of opinion whatsoever over the issue of not killing them, even if the person has reached maturity, this is because the person is not responsible by agreement. The evidence that these types of people (are not to be fought against) is the saying of Allāh,

"Fight in the way of Allāh against those who fight you and do not transgress the limits (set by Allāh). Indeed, Allāh does not love those who transgress."

{al-Baqarah (2): 190}

199

From these types of people are those who are generally unable to fight such as the elderly, the decrepit, those who are secluded in worship, hired workers, mothers and the likes who are not to be transgressed against during fighting and Allāh gave them a special position in that it is prohibited to kill them due to His saying,

"...and do not transgress the limits (set by Allāh)."

{al-Baqarah (2): 190}

Meaning: do not kill non-combatants such as women due to their inability to fight.

From Imām al-Mujtahid Abū 'Abdullāh Muhammad bin 'Īsā bin Muhammad bin Asbagh al-Azdī al-Qurtubī (aka Ibn Munāsif), eds. Muhammad bin Zakariyyā Abū Ghāzī and Shaykh Mashhūr Hasan Āl Salmān, *Kitāb ul-Injād fī Abwāb il-Jihād* (Beirut: Mu'assasah ar-Rayān, 1425 AH/2005 CE), vol.1, p.228.

96 See: http://www.salafimanhaj.com/pdf/SalafiManhaj_Fighting
See pp.18-20 for further detailed study of the hadeeth of the attack on Tā'if with *manjaneeq*.

97 Refer to lectures *'Politics in Light of Islam'* by Shaykh, Dr Khālid al-Anbarī at salafimanhaj.com

98 *Sunan Ibn Mājah*, vol.2, p.1008, hadeeth no.3029

99 *Sunan an-Nasā'ī*, vol.5, p.268, hadeeth no.3057

100 *Saheeh Ibn Khuzaymah*, vol.4, p.274, hadeeth no.2867

101 *Saheeh Ibn Hibbān*, vol.9, p.183, hadeeth no.3871

102 *Al-Mustadrak*, vol.1, p.466

103 http://www.islamicthinkers.com/index/index.php

104 *Majmoo' al-Fatāwā Ibn Bāz*, vol.6, p.525

105 From a Q&A session dated Sunday 14 April 2002 and broadcast on Paltalk.

106 http://uk.youtube.com/watch?v=ByCDp8TRKfI

107 http://uk.youtube.com/watch?v=XYWotvV7Qmk

108 Imām Tirmidhee adds, **"This hadeeth is hasan, it is narrated by more than one person from Sa'eed bin Jamhān..."** Refer to *Jāmi' at-Tirmidhī*, vol.4, p.436, *'Awn al-Ma'bood*, vol.12, p.260.

109 http://www.youtube.com/watch?v=ZBKhKK9ZWuo

¹¹⁰ Refer to this important *khutbah* on the *fiqh* of *al-Amr bi'l-Ma'roof wa'n-Nahy'an il-Munkar* by Shaykh Muhammad Sa'eed Raslān: http://www.rslan.com/vad/items_details.php?id=667

¹¹¹ There is an edit of this by A.A. Atā (Cairo, 1975) and a Beirut reprint in 1986 CE.

¹¹² Reported by al-Bukhārī in his *Saheeh*.

¹¹³ The prerequisites of a *Mujtahid* have been discussed within some of the early works of *fuqahā* (jurists) such as Abū Husays al-Basrī (436 AH/1044 CE) in *al-Mu'tamad fī Usūl il-Fiqh*. Also within the works of Sayfuddeen al-Āmidī in *al-Ihkām fī Usūl il-Ahkām* (Cairo: Subayh, 1968 CE), al-Ghazzālī, al-Isnawī, al-Baydāwī (685 AH/1286 CE) and Ibn ul-Humām (861 AH/1456 CE).

¹¹⁴ This has been dealt with by Imām ash-Shātibī (d.790 AH) in his work *al-Muwāfaqāt*.

¹¹⁵ See: http://www.islamicthinkers.com/index/index.php?option=com_content&task=view&id=629&Itemid=26

¹¹⁶ Reported by Abū Dāwood, at-Tirmidhī and Ibn Mājah and it is *Saheeh*.

¹¹⁷ Al-Lālikā'ī, *Sharh Usūl I'tiqād Ahl us-Sunnah*, vol.1, p.156

¹¹⁸ *Zād ul-Ma'ad*, vol.1, p.38

¹¹⁹ Allāh says:

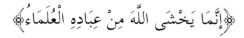

$$﴿إِنَّمَا يَخْشَى اللَّهَ مِنْ عِبَادِهِ الْعُلَمَاءُ﴾$$

"Those who only fear Allāh from among His servants, are the 'Ulama (those who have knowledge)."
{Fātir (35): 28}

Allāh says,

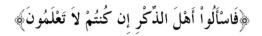

$$﴿فَاسْأَلُواْ أَهْلَ الذِّكْرِ إِن كُنتُمْ لاَ تَعْلَمُونَ﴾$$

"Ask the people of knowledge if you do not know"
{al-Anbiyā (16): 43}

Allāh says:

201

﴿وَإِذَا جَاءَهُمْ أَمْرٌ مِّنَ الأَمْنِ أَوِ الْخَوْفِ أَذَاعُواْ بِهِ وَلَوْ رَدُّوهُ إِلَى الرَّسُولِ وَإِلَى

أُوْلِي الأَمْرِ مِنْهُمْ لَعَلِمَهُ الَّذِينَ يَسْتَنبِطُونَهُ مِنْهُمْ وَلَوْلاَ فَضْلُ اللّهِ عَلَيْكُمْ وَرَحْمَتُهُ

لاَتَّبَعْتُمُ الشَّيْطَانَ إِلاَّ قَلِيلاً﴾

"And when there comes to them something (i.e. information) about (public) security or fear, they spread it around. But if they had only referred it back to the Messenger or to those of authority among them, then the ones who (can) draw correct conclusions from it would have known about it. And if not for the favour of Allāh upon you and His mercy, you would have followed Shaytān, except for a few of you."

{an-Nisā (4): 83}

[120] Saheeh Bukhārī and Muslim

[121] Ibn Mājah, Saheeh

[122] See: http://www.salafimanhaj.com/pdf/SalafiManhaj_Deception.pdf

[123] See: http://www.salafimanhaj.com/pdf/SalafiManhaj_Awlaki

[124] See: http://www.salafimanhaj.com/pdf/SalafiManhajQatādah.pdf

[125] See: http://www.salafimanhaj.com/pdf/SalafiManhaj_Tartoosee.pdf

[126] Reported by Abū Dāwood , ad-Dārimī, at-Tirmidhī and Ahmad

[127] Saheeh Muslim

[128] The evidence for the obligation of accepting *Khabr ul-Wāhid* in matters of creed are evidences which necessitate acting by the *Khabr ul-Wāhid*, and these are absolute in the general sense. Also there is no differentiation to be made between one matter and another or between one issue and another. Furthermore, rejecting *Khabr ul-Wāhid* necessitates rejecting much of the correct Islamic 'aqeedah. See Muhammad bin Husayn bin Hasan al-Jīzānī, *Ma'ālim Usūl ul-Fiqh 'inda Ahl is-Sunnah wa'l-Jama'ah* [Signposts of Islamic Legal Principles According to Ahl us-Sunnah wa'l-Jama'ah] (Dammām, KSA: Dār Ibn ul-Jawzī, 1428 AH/2007 CE), p.144.

So if this is well affirmed in *Usūl ul-Fiqh* how on earth did Omar Bakrī Muhammad, manage to construe for so many years that *Khabr ul-Āhād* should not be taken into matters of *'aqeedah?* Where did he get this understanding from? Indeed, further study indicates that he inherited this notion from the Mu'tazilah who were the only sect to not take the *Khabr ul-Āhād* into *'aqeedah*. So when Omar Bakrī was told about this throughout the 1990s why did he totally reject and stay in line with Mu'tazilah, only to then reject it later when it was political viable for his movement to take shape in rejecting it?

[129] Refer the following article:

http://www.islamicthinkers.com/index/index.php?option=com_content&task=view&id=478&Itemid=26

[130] This has been edited by Safwan 'Adnan Dawudi (Damascus: Dar al-Qalam, 1412 AH/1992 CE) and there are also: an edit in Damascus: Dar al-Qalam, 1997; an edit from Beirut: Dar al-Shamiyya, 1383 AH/1964 CE); Beirut: Dar al Ma'rifah, n.d.; an edit by Nadim Mar'ashli in 1984 printed by Dār ul-Kitāb il-Arabi in Beirut.

[131] For Anjem Choudhary's Yuppie image throughout the *al-Muhajiroun* phase of the cult in the mid 1990s refer to:

http://video.google.com/videoplay?docid=-2560493866437684563

[132] *Mughnī al-Muhtāj*, vol.4, p.375; al-Kāsānī, *Bidāi' as-Sinā'i*, vol.7, p.4; al-Khateeb, *Mukhtasar al-Jaleel*, vol.6, p.87.

[133] Ibn Qudāmah, *al-Mughnī*, vol.10, p.37

[134] Abū Dawūd, Nasā'ī, Ibn Mājah and at-Tirmidhi

[135] Ar-Ramlī, *Nihāyat ul-Muhtāj Sharh al-Minhāj*, vol.8, p.226; al-Bājee, *al-Muntaqā*, vol.5, p.188.

[136] See Ibn Qudāmah, *al-Mugnī*, vol.10, p.37; *an-Nihayāt ul-Muhtāj*, vol.8, p.326

[137] Ibn Rushd, *al-Bidāyah wa'n-Nihāyah*, vol.2, pp.383-384

[138] http://osolihin.files.wordpress.com/2007/03/jihad-and-methodology.pdf - see page 4

[139] This interview is available to view on *youtube*. Much of what Choudhary said in this interview was also repeated in his interview with Ian Collins of Talksport Radio at the end of March 2009 which can also be found Online. He again claims that the word 'Islam' is derived from the form-ten verb 'istislām' and claim that the Sharee'ah is not implemented anywhere in the world today. Interview with Ian Collins can be downloaded here: http://uploading.com/files/TJCRH8JP/Anjem

[140] Al-Bukhārī, *as-Saheeh, hadeeth* no.5752; Muslim, *as-Saheeh, hadeeth* no. 60

141 Al-Bukhārī, *as-Saheeh*, hadeeth no.48; Muslim, *as-Saheeh, hadeeth* no. 64

142 Reported by at-Tabarānī from the *hadeeth* of Hishām bin 'Urwah – *hadeeth* graded *Saheeh* by al-Albānī as in *Saheeh al-Jāmi' as-Sagheer* (1269).

143 Part 3 of the Press TV interview on *youtube*.

144 For more on this refer to paper by Dr Nāsir Ibrāheem al-Muhaimeed (Judge in the Appellate Court in Riyadh and Judicial Expert of the Arab league):

http://www.moj.gov.sa/adl/ENG/attach/85.pdf

145 For more on this refer to paper by Dr 'AbdurRahmān bin Nā'if as-Sulamī, *The Ordering of the Classes of Beneficiaries of Waqf in Islamic Jurisprudence: A Comparative Juristic Study Applied on a Deed of Endowment Issued by the High Court of Jeddah*:

http://www.moj.gov.sa/adl/ENG/attach/72.pdf

146 See *Saheeh al-Bukhārī, Book of Zakāt*, vol.2, p.530; and *Saheeh Muslim, Book of Zakāt*, vol.2, p.693.

147 Reported by al-Bukhārī, *Book of Wills and Testaments*, vol.3, p.1019 and Muslim, *Book of Wills*, vol.3, p.1255.

148 *Tafseer al-Qurtubī*, vol.6, p.339.

149 Reported by Ibn Qudāmah in *al-Mughnī*, vol.8, p.185 and Ibn Muflih in *al-Mubdi'*, vol.5, p.312.

150 *Mughnī al-Muhtāj*, vol.2, p.376.

151 Ibid.

152 *Sunan at-Tirmidhī, Book of Endowments*, vol.3, p.659 following *hadeeth* no. 1375.

153 For more on this refer to a paper by Dr 'AbdurRahmān bin Āyd Āl 'Āyd (Assistant Professor at the Department of Islamic Jurisprudence, Sharee'ah College, *Imam Muhammad bin Saud Islamic University*):

http://www.moj.gov.sa/adl/ENG/attach/104.pdf

154 For more on this refer to a paper by Dr 'Ali bin Rāshid ad-Dubayān (a judge with the Saudi Ministry of Justice): http://www.moj.gov.sa/adl/ENG/attach/74.pdf

155 *Al-Ifsāh*, vol.2, pp.267-268; *Bidāyat ul-Mujtahid*, vol.1, pp.471; and *Hilyat al-'Ulamā'*, vol.8, p.93.

156 Reported by Muslim, vol. 3, p.1588, *Book of Beverages*, hadeeth no. 75.

157 See *Fath al-Bārī 'alā Saheeh al-Bukhārī*, vol.10, p.48, *Book of Beverages*; and *Saheeh Muslim*, vol.4, p.4322, *Book of Tafseer*, hadeeth no. 33.

[158] Saheeh Muslim, vol.3, p.1570, *Book of Beverages*, hadeeth no. 3.

[159] For more on this refer to a paper by Dr Ahmad bin Sālih al-Barrāk: http://www.moj.gov.sa/adl/ENG/attach/58.pdf

[160] Saheeh al-Bukhārī, vol.4, p.1656, *hadeeth* no. 4277; Saheeh Muslim, vol.3, p.1335, *hadeeth* no. 1711.

[161] Saheeh al-Bukhārī, vol.2, p.889, *hadeeth* no. 2380; Saheeh Muslim, vol.1, p.122, *hadeeth* no. 138.

[162] This *hadeeth* was narrated by Abū Dāwūd, vol.3, p.305, *hadeeth* no. 3597; al-Hākim, vol.2, p.32, *hadeeth* no. 2222; and al-Bayhaqī in *as-Sunan al-Kubrā*, vol.6, p.82, *hadeeth* no. 11223. Imām al-Albānī categorized it as *saheeh* (authentic) in *Saheeh al-Jāmi'*, no. *6196 and As-Silsilah As-Saheehah*, no. 438.

[163] This *hadeeth* was narrated by Ibn Mājah, vol.2, p.778, *hadeeth* no. 2320; and al-Hākim, vol.4, p.111, *hadeeth* no. 7051; al-Hākim categorized it as Saheeh (authentic) and so did Imām adh-Dhahabī. Imām al-Albānī also categorized it as *Saheeh* (authentic) in *Saheeh Al-Jāmi'*, no. 6049.

[164] This *hadeeth* was narrated by al-Bayhaqī in *as-Sunan al-Kubrā*, vol.10, p.150, *hadeeth* no. 20324; ad-Dāraqutnī in *as-Sunan*, vol.4, pp.206, 16 and 2074; al-Bayhaqī in *Ma'rifat As-Sunan Wa'l-Āthār*, hadeeth no. 5873; al-Khateeb al-Baghdādī in *Tāreekh Baghdād*, vol.10, p.449; al-Hāfidh az-Zaila'ī in *Nasb ar-Rāyah*, vol.4, p.81; and al-Hāfidh Ibn 'AbdulBarr in *al-Istidhkār*, vol.7, p.103-4. al-Hāfidh Ibn 'AbdulBarr said,

> **This report has been narrated about 'Umar *(radi Allāhu 'anhu)* from various narrators from the Hejaz, Iraq, Syria and Egypt. Thank God for that.**

[165] *Imām As-Sarakhsī, Al-Mabsūt*, vol.16, p.63.

[166] An-Nawawī, *Sharh Saheeh Muslim*, vol.12, p.3.

[167] *Ibn Hisham* vol.1, pp.428-430.

[168] Ibid.

[169] *Ibn Hisham* vol.1, pp.435-438; vol.2, p.90, and *Zad ul-Ma'ad* vol.2, p.51.

[170] Edward Luttwak, Coup d'État: a Practical Handbook (Cambridge, MA: Harvard University Press, 1979), p.27. The book was originally published in 1968.

[171] This was compiled by 'AbdurRahmān bin Qāsim and was printed by Dār ul-Iftā', Riyadh and the second printing was in 1385 AH/1965 CE, while the fifth edition was

printed in 1413 AH/1992 CE, the sixth printing was in 1417 AH/1996 CE. There is also a print dated 1420 AH/1999CE.

[172] Shaykh 'Ali Hasan al-Halabī al-Atharī stated: This indicates that *Salāt ul-Janāzah* (the funeral prayer) is to be prayed in a *musalla* and not in a *Masjid*. It is permissible to pray *Salāt ul-Janāzah* in a *Masjid* but it is better if it is prayed in a *musalla* (a wide open area wherein the people go out to pray).

[173] In a class given at the *Imām al-Albānī Centre* 'Ammān, Jordan on Thursday 16th March 2006 CE

[174] Meaning: to rule with what Allāh has revealed.

[175] Hamza as-Sahmī, *Tāreekh Jurjān*, p.70.

[176] 'Jurjān' is the Arabic name for 'Gorgan' which is the capital city of the Golestan Province in Northern Iran and is south-east of the Caspian Sea.

[177] See vol.1, pp.166-68 with some slight additions to it.

[178] Ar-Rawdānī, *Sillatul-Khalaf bi-Mawsūl as-Salaf*, p.407, this text was overlooked by the editor of *al-Mu'jam*.

[179] *Sharh Hadeeth in-Nuzūl*, pp.51-2

[180] Ibid. and pp.9-10

[181] This book was overlooked by the editor Dr Ziyad Muhammad Mansūr in *al-Mu'jam*.

[182] *Fath ul-Bārī*, vol.1, p.292, vol.7, p.445, vol.8, p.218

[183] *Al-Bidāyah wa'n-Nihāyah*, vol.11, p.298

[184] In *Dhamm it-Ta'weel*, p.17

[185] The Arabic used here is *'Abnā'* which is an abridgement of *'Akhbaranā'* '(he informed us...').

[186] *Al-'Uluww*, p.167; *Tadhkiratul-Huffādh*, vol.3, p.449 and *Siyar*, vol.16, p.295

[187] *Mukhtasar al-'Uluww*, p.49

[188] *Al-Arba'een fī Sifāt Rabb ul-'Ālameen*, p.118.

[189] *Al-Arba'een fī Sifāt Rabb ul-'Ālameen*, p.118.

[190] *Fath ul-Bārī*, vol.1, p.105

[191] See al-Hāfidh Abī Bakr Ahmad bin Ibrāheem al-Ismā'īlī, Jamāl 'Azoon (ed.), intro. By Shaykh Hammād bin Muhammad al-Ansārī, *Kitāb I'tiqād Ahl is-Sunnah* (Riyadh, KSA: Dār Ibn Hazm, 1420 AH/1999 CE), pp.55-56.

¹⁹² Shaykh 'Ali Hasan al-Halabī al-Atharī stated: Some people make du'ā against the Muslim leaders or curse and slander them and this is not from the characteristics of the people of truth.

¹⁹³ Shaykh 'Ali Hasan al-Halabī al-Atharī stated:

> **This obviously means by extension removing themselves from the obedience of Allāh as the Prophet *(sallallāhu alayhi wassallam)* said *"There is no obedience to the creation in disobedience to the Creator"* and he *(sallallāhu alayhi wassallam)* also said *"Obedience is only in that which is good."* If the issue is in regards to that which opposes the Divine Legislation and the affair of the Allāh and His Messenger, then obedience in this regard is not permissible.**

¹⁹⁴ Meaning: responding in obedience to the leader is as if you have responded in obedience to Allāh, it is obligatory.

¹⁹⁵ Instead of making *du'ā* against them we make *du'ā* for them as Imām Ahmad *(rahimahullāh)* mentioned.

¹⁹⁶ Meaning: even if those Muslim rulers are sinners and transgressors.

¹⁹⁷ Shaykh 'Ali Hasan al-Halabī al-Atharī stated:

> **Here we must stop at this word "mutaghallib (the one who overpowers and becomes dominant)" for a while. In the next session it will be made apparent to us that the paths for a ruler acquiring power are numerous and from the paths are in the case of a ruler who becomes dominant and overpowers others *(al-Mutaghallib)*. It is when a person opposes the Divine Legislation and revolts against the Muslim leader and thus becomes dominant, and this has happened in Islamic history and the scholars noted that this opposes the Divine Legislation. However, the one who revolted against the Muslim ruler has established and settled security and command now and is able to control the Muslim lands as he obviously is a Muslim yet has opposed the consensus of the Muslims by revolting in the first place yet has seized the reins of power from the first bearers of it. The scholars have reached agreement that the leader who overpowers the reins of authority**

from another leader is to be obeyed and this is Divine Legislated. Why? Because it is feared that revolting against this one again will only cause a worse tribulation. For that reason, the greatest intents of the Divine Legislation is that preventing the harms takes precedence over enforcing the benefit.

[198] Shaykh 'Ali Hasan al-Halabī al-Atharī stated:

As now the leader would have been expelled from the condition of being a Muslim due to falling into clear *kufr*. For this reason, the Prophet *(sallallāhu alayhi wassallam)* said: *"Until you see clear (buwāhan) kufr, for which you have with you evidence from Allāh."* Pay attention here: *"you have with you ('indakum)"* meaning that this evidence is firmly settled in you hearts and is clear in front of your eyes, not any type of *kufr* rather it must be clear, explicit and apparent!

[199] See *Sharh Saheeh Muslim*, vol.12, p.229

[200] Shaykh 'Ali Hasan al-Halabī al-Atharī stated: *"Bayah'nā Rasullullāh..."* means: that we are the ones who pledge allegiance to the Messenger, we are the doers and the messenger of Allāh is the *maf'ul bihi*. But if we say *"Bayyah'nā Rasulullāh"* means that we are the *maf'ul-bihi* and the messenger of Allāh is the one who made bay'ah to us.

[201] Shaykh 'Ali Hasan al-Halabī al-Atharī stated:

Meaning that they have the authority, power and ability of command and to implement and rule according to it. it is not a mere saying and for this reason the Muslims who currently dwell in the West, what do we say to them? We say to them that is not permissible to instigate chaos, revolt and agitation and we do not say this in thinking that such rulers (in the West) are Muslims as they are neither Muslims nor do they say that they are Muslims however the greater benefit is not to cause destabilisation and agitation in those countries, not to mention in the Muslims countries aswell, does not bequeath anything except for tribulation, inquisition, calamity which is not known except by the Lord of the Worlds.

²⁰² Shaykh 'Ali Hasan al-Halabī al-Atharī stated:

> In regards to the *hadeeth* about *"whoever sees an evil then let him change it with his hand, or with his tongue (by speaking) or with his heart"* then changing with the heart is for the common people and likewise their rejection is via their hearts. As for changing the evil by speaking then this is for the scholars and the people of knowledge. Another *hadeeth* which was authenticated by our Shaykh (i.e. Imām al-Albānee, *rahimahullāh*) and makes clear that advice to the ruler differs from advice to the common people, wherein the Prophet *(sallallāhu alayhi wassallam)* said *"Whoever has advice for the Muslim ruler then he should not be given openly, rather it should be done privately."*

²⁰³ When Husayn *(radi Allāhu 'anhu)* said that he wanted to go they told him not to go.

²⁰⁴ Meaning: before he went out they said "you will be killed."

²⁰⁵ Shaykh 'Ali stated:

> Also, we neither throw doubts on the intentions of Husayn nor do we throw doubt upon his desire to spread the deen and we do not throw doubt on his safeguarding that which is more complete and better. However, is it from the conditions that he (radi Allāh 'anhu) will not be mistaken? What happened, happened, which indicated that he (radi Allāhu 'anhu) was not correct in that matter.

²⁰⁶ Therefore, his intention in revolting was what? To establish good and ward off evil.

²⁰⁷ Meaning: to intend corruption.

²⁰⁸ He wants rectification yet does not realise it.

²⁰⁹ Hasan, the brother of Husayn, Husayn revolted so Hasan was better.

²¹⁰ The *hadeeth* is in Bukhārī.

²¹¹ For both and Arabic and English texts see *Foundations of the Sunnah by Imām Ahmad ibn Hanbal* (Birmingham: Salafi Publications, 1417 AH/1997 CE), pp.37-38

²¹² *Majmū' ar-Rasā'il wa'l-Masā'il*, vol.5, p.199

²¹³ See Ismā'īl bin Yahyā al-Muzanī, Jamāl 'Azoon (ed.), *Kitāb Sharh us-Sunnah* (Riyadh, KSA: Dār Ibn Hazm, 1420 AH/2000 CE), p.85.

209

214 He was the one who tested all of the scholars of his time with saying that the Qur'ān was created, he wrote to his deputies and threatened the scholars. Most of the scholars went along with the heretical creed out of fear except for Ahmad ibn Hanbal and Muhammad ibn Nooh, they were both chained and sent to be tried by al-Ma'moon who was in Tarsūs (currently in Turkey), but al-Ma'moon died before their arrival. Adh-Dhahabī, *Duwal al-Islām*, p.132

215 He also tested the people with the creed of the Qur'ān being created and wrote to the different lands saying that this should be the creed. See *Siyar 'A'lam un-Nubalā*, vol.10, p.291

216 He tested the people with the creed of the Qur'ān being created also during 231 AH, during this time Ahmad ibn Nasr al-Khazā'ī was executed for refusing to give into the heretical creed. See adh-Dhahabī, *Duwal al- Islām*, p.139

217 He revived the *Sunnah* and killed the innovation of the creed of the Qur'ān being created. See ibid., p.149

218 The descriptions of these notable are taken from the book *Duwal ul-Islām* by adh-Dhahabee

219 Adh-Dhahabī, *Siyar*, vol.12, p.492

220 From his book *al-'Azeez* which was his commentary of *al-Wajeez* of al-Ghazālī, it is also known as *as-Sharh ul-Kabeer*.

221 As-Suyūṭī, *Hasanul-Muhādhirah*, vol.1, p.399. Al-Isnawee in vol.1, p.44 said "I do not know the date of her death". It is worth brining to attention here two relatives of al-Muzanī:

First: ar-Rabī' bin Sulaymān al-Murādī, the brother of al-Muzanī via suckling (having suckled from the same woman as babies). Adh-Dhahabī reports in *Siyar*, vol.12, p.392 with a chain of transmission to Abi'l-Fawāris as-Sindī saying **"al-Muzanī died in 264 AH and ar-Rabī' died in 270 AH"**, adh-Dhahabī said **"Between their suckling at birth was six months"**.

Second: His nephew, at-Tahāwī, the famous Imām and author of *al-'Aqeedah Tahāwiyyah*.

222 Soon will come some speech regarding the influence of Imām Shāfi'ī on al-Muzanī.

223 A resident of Egypt and one of its senior Imāms, he narrated from Muhammad bin al-Hasan *al-Jāmi' al-Kabeer* and *al-Jāmi' as-Sagheer*. He died in 218 AH, see *Siyar 'A'lam un-Nubalā'*, vol.10, p.631

224 Ibn Mu'awiyah al-Khazā'ī, the Imām, *Allāmah, Hāfidh*, he arrived in Egypt and did not leave it until al-Mu'tasim presided over it and thus he was asked about the Qur'ān being created and he refused to answer with what al-Mu'tasim wanted. He was imprisoned in Sāmarā' where he remained until death in 228 AH. See *Siyar*, vol.10, p.595. Al-Muzanī was asked about his beliefs about the Qur'ān and narrations, as will be mentioned shortly.

225 Ibn Sa'eed bin Nāfi' Abū 'Abdullāh al-Umawī al-Misrī al-Mālikī, he died in 225 AH. See *Siyar*, vol.10, pp.656-58

226 His history has not lost its precious heritage and nothing of it exists except for transmissions of praise in biographies. See the book by Dr. Bashhār 'Awwād on adh-Dhahabī and his methodology in the book *Tāreekh ul-Islām*, p.234 wherein he mentions among the publications his abridgement of Ibn Yoonus' *Tāreekh*.

227 *Wafayāt ul-'A'yān*, vol.1, p.218

228 *Siyar*, vol.12, p.493 with a chain of transmission back to him and that which is in *Tabaqāt ul-Fuqahā*, p.89 of ash-Shīrāzī: "A proof of the detailed meanings..."

229 Al-Bayhaqī, *Manāqib ush-Shāfi'ī*, vol.2, p.351, with an *isnād* back to him.

230 Ibid., vol.2, p.351

231 *Tabaqāt ul-Fuqahā ush-Shāfi'iyyah*, p.9

232 *Al-Intiqā' fī Fadā'il ath-Thalāthatil-A'immah il-Fuqahā*, p.110

233 *Al-Muntadham*, vol.12, p.192

234 *Wafayāt ul-'A'yān*, vol.1, p.218

235 *Siyar*, vol.12, p.492

236 *Tabaqāt ush-Shāfi'iyyah al-Kubrā*, vol.1, p.238

237 *Tabaqāt ush-Shāfi'iyyah*, vol.1, p.34

238 Ibn Abi'l-'Izz al-Hanafī in *Sharh ut-Tahāwiyyah*, p.370 mentions:

Having obedience to them (the leaders), even if they oppress, because revolting against them will result in greater corruptions than their oppression. Rather, to be patient with their transgression absolves one from evil actions and multiplies the rewards. Allāh has only placed such leaders over us due to our corrupt actions so the results are from the actions being done, so it is for us to strive in seeking forgiveness from Allāh and to repent and rectify our actions...**So if the people want to be free from the oppression of the oppressive leader they have to leave off oppression themselves.**"

239 Shaykh 'Ali Hasan al-Halabī al-Atharī stated:

If such a person is a disbeliever who is outside the fold of the religion then the issue of revolting against him is not something that would need to be researched at all. The issue of revolting against a non-Muslim ruler has to be referred back to weighing up between the benefits and harms and it also has to be referred back to the *fatāwā* of the scholars.

240 Shaykh 'Ali Hasan al-Halabī al-Atharī stated: To the extent that Imām Ahmad ibn Hanbal *(rahimahullāh)* would say **"If my du'ā would be accepted, I would make du'ā for the sultān (governer/ruler)"**, as if the ruler is rectified then so would the people under him and also the affairs of the society.

241 i.e., the people of *hadeeth* who are the saved sect and the aided group.

242 See translaton: Abū 'Uthmān Ismā'eel ibn 'AbdurRahmān as-Sābūnī, *'Aqeedat us-Salaf wa As-hāb ul-Hadeeth* [The Creed of the Pious Predecessors and the People of Hadeeth], London: Brixton Mosque Islamic Centre, 1420 AH/1999 CE, pp.93-4.

243 For both and Arabic and English texts see *Foundations of the Sunnah by Imām Ahmad ibn Hanbal* (Birmingham: Salafi Publications, 1417 AH/1997 CE), pp.37-38

244 The book is available for purchase here: http://www.lawbooks-online.com/index.asp?title=Essential+Fiqh&isbn=&match type=exact&search=simple&imageField.x=0&imageField.y=0

245 The scholars of *hadeeth* have noted that there are five main types of *tadlees*:

1. *Tadlees ul-Isnad* – this where a narrator claims to have heard a *hadeeth* or a narration from a Shaykh who he usually narrates from and studies with, but in this case he did not hear anything at all from the Shaykh. There is a degree of meeting and correspondence yet in this case he ascribes something to the Shaykh which he did not actually directly hear from him. Ibn 'AbdulBarr *(rahimahullāh)* states **"As for tadlees it is when a man narrates from a man who he met and lived in the same time as and took from him and narrates from the man what he did not directly heard from him"**, *at-Tamheed*, vol.1, pp.15-16. So here the narrator will say **"Anna"** (certainly...), **"'an"** (from...) or **"Qāla"** (he said) so it is not necessarily a clear and blatant lie.

2. *Tadlees ut-Taswiyah* – this is the most serious type as it is when a narrator purposefully leaves out and drops someone in his chain of transmission because he is weak and it will weaken his narrations. So for example, a Shaykh who is *thiqah* heard from one who was weak who heard from one who is *thiqah*, yet the weak one is dropped and left out of the chain in order to make it seem as if the two *thiqāt* heard directly from each other without anyone in the middle.

3. *Tadlees ul-Qat'* – this when the narrator of a *hadeeth* pauses and then just mentions any name as if the name mentioned actually relayed the *hadeeth*. This is also known as *Tadlees us-Sukūt*.

4. *Tadlees ul-'Atf* – this is when a narrator narrates from 2 Shaykhs but actually only heard from one of them.

5. *Tadlees ush-Shuyūkh* – this is when a narrator uses a name of a person in a chain of narration that is well known by the people as being credible, when in reality it is a person who is da'eef but with the same name. So for example, the *mudallis* states **"I heard Abū 'Abdullāh say..."** trying to deceive the people that it is Ahmad ibn Hanbal who is well known for the name "Aboo 'Abdullāh" when it is really someone else. Or using "Abū Sālih" will be used for Ahmad ibn Hanbal in order to make it seem as if the narrator if narrating from someone else so as not to be repetitive in narrating from Ahmad ibn Hanbal. Al-Khateeb al-Baghdādī states in *al-Kifāyah* (p. 365) that **"...it is where a muhaddith narrates from a Shaykh who he heard from yet changes his name, kunyah or nisba or alters his well known condition to one which is unknown."** This is prevalent today especially with the explosion of the worldwide web and internet forums wherein people use false names, hide behind false identities and use fake pseudonyms. In any case in the modern era it is still practiced in relation to knowledge and Omar Bakrī Muhammad Fustuq is the best example of contemporary *tadlees*. Not only did he claim to study in *Umm ul-Qura'* and the *Islamic University of Madeenah* but he also claimed to study with "az-Zuhaylī", insinuating by this the famous Wahbah az-Zuhaylī. But when one of the brothers in London went to Syria in the late 1990s and asked Wahbah az-Zuhaylī directly if Omar Bakrī was his student

Shaykh Zuhaylī denied even knowing Bakrī. When Bakrī was confronted over this, Bakrī said **"No, no, not that Zuhaylī, another Zuhaylī"**!! Clear *tadlees*!

246 http://osolihin.files.wordpress.com/2007/03/jihad-and-methodology.pdf

247 See 'AbdurRahmān ibn Muhammad Sa'eed Dimashqiyyah, *Hizb ut-Tahreer* (Istanbool, Turkey: Maktabah al-Ghurabā', 1417 AH/1997CE), pp.63-66.

248 We have also found an Arabic transcript of the story that was picked up in *ash-Sharq al-Awsat* (London), by Muhammad ash-Shāfi'ī (Mohammed Shafey), dated: Yawm ul-Ahad 2nd Shawwāl 1428 AH/Sunday October 14th 2007 CE. Refer to the Arabic article here:

http://www.āwsat.com/details.asp?section=4&issue=10547&article=441214&search =عرم%20كبري&state=true

249 It can also be seen here:

http://www.manār.com/vb/showthread.php?p=44685
http://www.manār.com/vb/showthread.php?t=15682

250 He should ask the question to himself, it is as if he has amnesia!!? See here for an example of maybe some of the reasons why he is going through what he is going through, **here he claims that the majority opinion is that even children of the non-Muslims are not innocent as this is only for the Muwahhiddeen; he also refers to the "magnificent 19"; praises Abū Musab az-Zarqāwī and makes takfeer of King Fahd:** http://www.youtube.com/watch?v=guQhWjm6d08

More importantly, Allāh says,

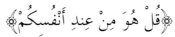

"Say it is from yourselves (i.e. due to your sin)..."
{Āli-'Imrān (3): 165}

And Allāh says,

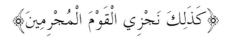

"Thus do We recompense the criminal people."
{Yūnus (10): 13}

214

And Allāh says,

$$﴿ظَهَرَ الْفَسَادُ فِي الْبَرِّ وَالْبَحْرِ بِمَا كَسَبَتْ أَيْدِي النَّاسِ لِيُذِيقَهُم بَعْضَ الَّذِي عَمِلُوا لَعَلَّهُمْ يَرْجِعُونَ﴾$$

"Corruption has appeared throughout the land and sea by [reason of] what the hands of people have earned so He may let them taste part of [the consequence of] what they have done that perhaps they will return [to righteousness]."

{Rūm (30): 41}

And Allāh says,

$$﴿وَمَا أَصَابَكُم مِّن مُّصِيبَةٍ فَبِمَا كَسَبَتْ أَيْدِيكُمْ وَيَعْفُو عَن كَثِيرٍ﴾$$

"And whatever strikes you of disaster – it is for what your hands have earned; but he pardons much."

{ash-Shūrā (42): 30}

---

[251] http://www.asharq-e.com/news.asp?section=3&id=9924

[252] We have demonstrated throughout this study that Omar Bakrī is not Salafi in any shape or form.

[253] La Hawla wa la Quwwata ila billāh! This is nonsense, let's refer to *The Devil's Deception of Abdullah Faysal ("Sheikh Faisal")* at: http://www.salafimanhaj.com/pdf/SalafiManhaj_Deception.pdf

[254] Hence, his intense desire to return to the UK and participate in the place where he really thinks "the da'wah among Muslims is stronger"!? This shows his love-hate relationship with the UK.

[255] It was okay however for him to take money in the form of the *DSS* (the UK welfare system) and to also receive abundant health care and treatment from the *NHS* (the UK National Health Service)!?

215

256 See his lecture pre 7/7 here for example: http://www.youtube.com/watch?v=JLh4xka1kSQ and also here: http://www.youtube.com/watch?v=zOv5X18SD9w

257 See Nafeez Mosaddeq Ahmed, *The London Bombings: An Independent Inquiry* (London: Duckworth, 2006), pp.54-55.

258 See Ahmed, *op.cit.*, pp.58-59

259 Ahmed, *op.cit.*, p.72

260 See Ahmed, *op.cit.*,p.76

261 Ahmed, *op.cit.*,p.82

262 Narrated by Mu'awiyah ibn Abī Sufyān *(radi Allāhu 'anhu)* in Bukhārī and Muslim; narrated by 'Abdullāh ibn 'Amr ibn al-'Ās *(radi Allāhu 'anhu)* in Saheeh Muslim; also in Abū Dāwūd.

263 Shaykh 'AbdulMālik bin Ahmad bin al-Mubārak Ramadānī al-Jazā'irī, *Fatāwā al-'Ulamā al-Akābir fimā Uhdira min Dimā fi'l-Jazā'ir* [The Legal Verdicts of the Senior Scholars Regarding the Killings in Algeria] - (Cairo: Dār Imam Ahmad, 1426 AH/2005 CE), pp.16-17.

264 Due to it applying the *Sharee'ah*.

265 Due to it exemplifying the correct understanding of Islām.

266 Even though they differed with most of the *Salafi manhaj* and *'aqeedah*.

267 From Shaykh 'AbdusSalām bin Sālim bin Rajā' as-Sihaymī (Associate Professor in the Department of Fiqh, College of Sharee'ah, Islamic University of Madeenah), *Kun Salafian 'alā'l-Jādah!* [Be a Serious Salafi!] (Cairo: Dār ul-Manhaj, 1426 AH/2005). With introductions by Shaykh 'Ali bin Muhammad bin Nāsir al-Faqīhī and Shaykh 'Ubayd bin 'Abdullāh al-Jābirī.

268 The dangerous statements of Omar Bakrī, which he denies when on Arabic and Western media, are enough to indicate his departure from the way of the Salafi scholars. See the following wherein the statements of the main Salafi scholars of the era on such issues are very clear: http://www.salafimanhaj.com/pdf/SalafiManhaj_Terrorism_In_KSA.pdf http://www.salafimanhaj.com/pdf/SalafiManhaj_Deception.pdf http://www.salafimanhaj.com/pdf/SalafiManhaj_TakfeerAndBombing.pdf